High-tech fragrance
OXYGEN MASK
for stress reduction

Sunidhi Bhargava

M.D IN TEXTILE DESIGN AND ASSISTANT PROFESSOR

notionpress
.com

INDIA · SINGAPORE · MALAYSIA

ISBN 979-8-89777-155-4

Price - Rs. 249/-

Abstract

Medical textiles are specialized materials used in healthcare to improve patient outcomes, comfort, and healing by interacting with the human body. They are made from natural or synthetic fibers and are subject to strict safety regulations. Medical textiles are used in wound care, surgery, infection control, drug delivery systems, and even as support frameworks in implants or artificial joints. They fall into categories like sanitary textiles, implantable textiles, and non-implantable textiles. Stress is a natural part of life that shapes experiences, tests resilience, and calls us to adapt. It is not the absence of stress that defines strength, but the ability to harness it and learn from it. Stress is the body's nonspecific response to any demand made upon it, orchestrated across all cells and tissues to mobilize energy to support vital functions. Over decades of research, accumulating data has started to bridge the physiological and psychological realms of stress, creating a unified picture.

Stress can have significant psychological and physiological effects on individuals, including psychological disorders, anxiety, depression, and chronic health issues. Childhood and adolescent stressors like violence, abuse, and divorce/marital conflict can lead to psychological disorders, personality disorders, and poor school performance. Traumatic events are highly prevalent in the general population, with estimates ranging from 40% to 70%. Acute Stress Disorder (ASD) and PTSD are two primary diagnoses related to trauma, with PTSD affecting 1 in 12 adults at some time in their life. Stress-related health issues have increased in recent years, including cardiovascular disease, mental health disorders, autoimmune diseases, digestive issues, and sleep disorders. Effective strategies for managing stress include mindfulness, meditation, exercise, sleep hygiene, time management, social support, and seeking professional help when overwhelmed. Engaging in meaningful social connections can provide emotional support and help reduce stress.

Introduction-

A specific subset of textile materials utilized in the healthcare sector for medical purposes are known as medical textiles. These textiles are meant to enhance patient outcomes, offer comfort, and aid in healing by interacting directly or indirectly with the human body. Medical textiles have a broad range of uses, including prosthetics, orthotics, surgical drapes, wound care goods, and hygiene items. By attending to the unique requirements of patients, healthcare providers, and medical settings, they make a substantial contribution to the healthcare industry. Materials created from synthetic or natural fibers and specifically designed for medical applications are known as medical textiles. They are appropriate for a range of medical applications due to their special qualities, which include breathability, moisture-wicking capacity, antibacterial effects, and biocompatibility. Medical textiles, in contrast to regular textiles, are subject to strict safety regulations that guarantee they won't injure people while they're being used. Wound care, surgery, infection control, drug delivery systems, and even serving as a support framework in implants or artificial joints are just a few of the many medical uses for these fabrics. They fall into a number of categories, including sanitary textiles, implantable textiles, and non-implantable textiles. While implantable textiles, like sutures or vascular grafts, are made to be directly integrated into the body, non-implantable textiles are utilized in things like bandages, dressings, and drapes.

Natural fibers like cotton, silk, and wool, or synthetic fibers like polyester, nylon, and polypropylene, or a combination of the two, can be used to make medical textiles. While synthetic fibers are frequently utilized for their durability, simplicity of manufacture, and versatility, natural fibers are preferred in particular applications because of their comfort and hypoallergenic qualities. Medical textiles frequently receive unique treatments to improve their qualities in addition to the fiber choices. For instance, hydrophilic therapies can assist in regulating moisture levels, while antibacterial treatments are used to prevent infection. Biocompatibility is a crucial characteristic of medicinal textiles. Medical textiles must not irritate or produce an immunological reaction since they frequently come into direct contact with delicate bodily tissues. Because of their biocompatibility, these materials can be used for extended periods of time without endangering the patient. The capacity to create a moisture-controlled atmosphere is another crucial component, as it is essential for encouraging wound healing or guaranteeing patient comfort. To lower the risk of infection, advanced wound dressings, for instance, may contain materials that wick away moisture while keeping the wound site dry.

Medical textiles are essential in healthcare for various applications, including wound care, surgical textiles, prosthetics and orthotics, infection control, drug delivery, and implantable textiles. They are used in bandages, dressings, and wraps to protect wounds, maintain sterile conditions during surgery, cover prosthetic limbs for comfort and functionality, and are often treated with antimicrobial agents to reduce infection risks. They also serve as vehicles for controlled drug delivery, releasing medication gradually over time. Additionally, medical textiles are crucial for implantable devices like vascular grafts and surgical sutures.

Biocompatibility is a crucial characteristic of medicinal textiles. Medical textiles must not irritate or produce an immunological reaction since they frequently come into direct contact with delicate bodily tissues. Because of their biocompatibility, these materials can be used for extended periods of time without endangering the patient. The capacity to create a moisture-controlled atmosphere is another crucial component, as it is essential for encouraging wound healing or guaranteeing patient comfort. To lower the risk of infection, advanced wound dressings, for instance, may contain materials that wick away moisture while keeping the wound site dry.

Review of literature -

Medical textiles are specialized materials made for use in medical applications that support or improve people's health and well-being. They are engineered with specific properties to provide therapeutic benefits, prevent infection, promote healing, and offer support in both clinical and everyday environments. Unlike conventional textiles, medical textiles must meet strict safety, comfort, and functionality standards. Examples of medical textiles include orthopedic supports, wound dressings, surgical garments, and even wearable health monitoring devices. Advanced composites, natural fibers, or synthetic materials can be used to create medical textiles, and their designs may include antimicrobial agents, sensors, or other active features to increase their efficacy in healthcare settings. A distinct class of textiles created especially for medical uses are known as medical textiles. Both therapeutic and diagnostic applications for these textiles are found in the healthcare industry. Medical textiles are used in anything from surgical gowns to wound care products and even prosthetics, and their main purpose is to support, protect, and comfort patients in medical settings.

Medical textiles are materials or textiles used for their diagnostic, therapeutic, or protective qualities in a variety of medical professions. They might be knitted, woven, or nonwoven textiles with extra qualities including flexibility, biocompatibility, and antimicrobial resistance that are crucial for medical applications.

Medical textile types include:

> **Textiles Made of Woven Materials:** These fabrics are strong and long-lasting because they are made by weaving threads together. They are frequently seen in drapes and surgical gowns.

> **Knitted Textiles:** Compression stockings, bandages, and therapeutic apparel can all be made from knitted materials since they are flexible and stretchable.

> **Nonwoven Textiles:** Instead of weaving or knitting, these are made by attaching fibres together. Disposable medical supplies like masks, gowns, and wound dressings are frequently made from nonwovens.

Smart textiles are sophisticated textiles that have electronics or sensors built into them. Vital sign monitoring or therapeutic effects, like pressure monitoring for wound healing, can be provided via these.

Chapter 1:

Features of medical textile -

- **Biocompatibility:** By minimizing any potential negative reactions when these fabrics come into contact with skin or biological fluids, they are made to be compatible with the human body.

- **Antimicrobial Properties:** In order to prevent infections in surgical or hospital environments, many medical fabrics are designed to withstand microbial development.

- **Water resistance and absorbency:** While some textiles used in medical applications, like wound dressings, are made to be waterproof or water-resistant, others are frequently made to absorb biological fluids.

- **Comfort and Durability:** Medical fabrics must be able to endure frequent washings, sterilizations, and use without losing their efficacy. Another important factor is comfort, particularly for products that will be in close contact with the skin.

- **Sterility:** To avoid infection, a lot of medical textiles are sterilized before usage. This is particularly crucial for goods.

- Customization: Depending on the medical need, medical textiles are frequently made to fit certain uses, with different degrees of strength, elasticity, and stretchability.

In ancient times, a mystical loom, known as Alethea, was crafted by the goddess Aetheria, the goddess of healing, wisdom, and balance of life. Aetheria had the power to weave materials from the essence of health and vitality, altering their strength, elasticity, and stretchability to meet the unique needs of mortals. These fabrics, blessed with the goddess's magic, could heal wounds, soothe pain, and restore lost vitality. The loom was not ordinary, and it was said to be used only by those with pure intentions. It was known to have three distinct types: the Thread of Resilience, the Elastic Veil of Restoration, and the Gossamer of Healing. The Thread of Resilience was a strong fabric, while the Elastic Veil of Restoration was an elasticity-imbued fabric that bind wounds and injuries, providing emotional comfort. The Gossamer of Healing was a delicate, breathable fabric with potent healing properties, used for complex medical needs like skin grafts or recovery from severe burns. The story of Aetheria's loom has inspired those seeking to blend ancient wisdom with modern medicine, with modern medical textiles serving specific needs tailored for healing and comfort.

The combination of medical sciences and textile technology created a new industry that is in charge of creating innovative materials that can improve the discomfort of patients' days. It was this combination that led to the term "medical textile." Medical textiles are now used for a wide range of patient care products, such as dressings, implanted surgical devices, bed linens, and personal protective equipment, among many other things. This is because their applications have expanded daily. Medical textiles can be defined in a variety of ways. A definition that is commonly employed is "manufactured goods, including textile products used in healthcare and hygiene, as well as surgical uses." "Fiber-based products and structures used in first aid or the clinical treatment of a wound or medical condition "The combination of medical sciences and textile technology created a new industry that is in charge of creating innovative materials that can improve the discomfort of patients' days. Fisher characterized medical textiles as the result of this mix. Medical textiles are defined as "a general term which describes a textile structure which has been designed and produced for use in any of a variety of medical applications, including implantable applications". Both natural and synthetic fibres are used to make medical textiles, with the type of fibre used depending on the particular end-use qualities required. Although natural resources will be the primary focus of this chapter, we will first go over a detailed classification of medical textiles in general. Medical textiles actually have a wide variety of product categories, segments, sub-segments, and sub-sub-segments. Depending on the intended use, these products are available in a vast array of different sizes, shapes, combinations, and requirements. The health care and hygiene products segment is broken down into these many applications, which range from sophisticated operating room attire to complicated knitted fabric for an artificial vascular graft, or simply a simple band-aid to a bioabsorbable. These products, which include pillowcases and adult incontinence supplies, are designed to be either cleaned or thrown away after only one usage. Generally speaking, the purpose of hygiene products is to make life easier and better.

1.1 **Overview of Stress**: Definition, causes, and different types of stress (acute, chronic, environmental, psychological, etc.).

- Dysphoros, a Titan, was the embodiment of stress and a powerful force that could both fortify and unravel life. Born from the union of Kleos, the god of glory, and Nykos, the goddess of night, Dysphoros was a force that could motivate but also tear down. The gods initially drawn to Dysphoros' power, as it could push mortals to achieve great feats or build vast empires. However, they soon realized that Dysphoros was a fickle force that could drain the energy and resolve of even the mightiest warriors and rulers.

1   Dysphoros had many forms, each a different aspect of his nature. His influence could be brief or eternal, and it took many shapes. Acute stress, a sudden burst of energy, was the first face of Dysphoros, providing clarity and alertness before war. Chronic stress, an unending storm, was caused by long-term worries or daily struggles, slowly eroding physical and mental health. Environmental stress, tied to the world itself, was felt in the very air mortals breathed.

2   Psychological stress, the most complex and subtle form of Dysphoros, was invisible and carried within the mind, twisted thoughts and emotions. It was often the most destructive form of stress, as it eroded the soul itself. Aias, a mighty warrior, experienced the full force of Dysphoros in battle but eventually learned to channel acute stress for short bursts of power and combat the long-term effects of chronic stress through rest and self-reflection.

3   Dysphoros' legacy is that stress is a natural part of life, shaping experiences, testing resilience, and calling us to adapt. It is not the absence of stress that defines strength, but the ability to harness it and learn from it.

Although the most of us will never come into contact with a mountain lion, we have all been in stressful situations or felt "stressed out." Think about a time when you were in a stressful circumstance. How did it affect your physical, emotional, and mental well-being? Since stress is a subjective emotion and is therefore "personal," it might imply various things to different people. However, we need a scientifically feasible definition to begin with in order to investigate it from a biological standpoint.

Biomedical perspective

Hans Selye, the founder of stress research, defined stress as the body's nonspecific response to any demand made upon it. Stressors, such as extreme heat or cold, starvation, obesity, injury, or threats to one's well-being, can cause a temporary increase in stress. Allostasis, which means achieving stability through change, includes mechanisms that maintain life-sustaining functions and promote adaptation to challenge and expand survival capabilities.

Stress is the body's stereotyped physiological response to a stimulus, orchestrated across all cells and tissues to mobilize energy to support vital functions. The broad physiological response largely remains the same regardless of the specific stressor that initiated it. Over decades of research, accumulating data has started to bridge the physiological and psychological realms of stress, creating a unified picture. The concept of being 'stressed out', or allostatic (over)load or toxic stress, is a concept that refers to the negative aspects of a stress response. Understanding the physiological and psychological realms of stress is crucial for understanding the physiology of the stress response

Functions that support the stress response

Stress can cause alterations in brain connections, pupil dilatation, rapid breathing, metabolic changes, elevated heart rate and blood pressure, shaking, and constricted blood vessels. Reduced production of saliva and digestive enzymes results from the slowing down of non-essential processes like digesting, renal filtration, and reproduction. Additionally, food passes more slowly through the intestines, and enough stress may cause stress diarrhoea or the spilling of intestinal contents. During a public speech, this can be similar to having a dry mouth.

Stressor classification

According to our concept, stressors might be any number of stimuli or events that cause an organism to deviate from its homeostatic range. This section will examine the classification of stressors and provide instances of each.

Three primary stressor domains are identified:

The modality in which a stressor appears is referred to as its origin or type. These can be social, psychological, or bodily. Duration refers to the length of time that a stressor persists. Acute stressors typically last anywhere from a few minutes to several hours. Chronic stresses can last anywhere from weeks to years, whereas sub chronic stressors might endure for days. Acute, sub chronic, and chronic stressors all cause the same initial stress response; but, once the stressor becomes a sustained event, things change. A minor, moderate, or large life-threatening event is characterized by its severity. These can be classified as mild, moderate, severe, or traumatic.

Stressors that are physical

Physical activity or exposure to harsh climatic conditions—such as competing in a bike race or experiencing excessive heat or cold—are examples of acute physical stresses. Predator-prey interactions are a classic example in the animal kingdom. Getting a severe injury, like a broken arm, is another. persistent illnesses and obesity/starvation (i.e., deviating from the homeostatic body weight set point) are examples of persistent physical stressors. Chronic physical stress also includes extended exposure to harsh surroundings. For instance, continuing to live at a high altitude requires the body to adjust to the reduced supply of oxygen.

Stressors on the mind

When asked to name examples of stress, most people think of psychological stressors, which are the most prevalent kinds of stressors for us modern humans. These vary in severity and can also be categorized as acute or chronic.

It's interesting to note that these stressors usually stem from worries or thoughts of a possible perceived threat, yet they all cause the same physiological reactions that are meant to help the body function at its best when it must fight, run, or freeze. This group of stressors includes everyday occurrences like fighting with a coworker or stuck in traffic, as well as more significant ones like divorce, bereavement, or concerns about one's finances and job.

Social stressors

Supportive social ties can serve as an efficient stress response buffer, but social interactions can be a powerful source of stresses for highly sociable species, The severity of these can also vary. The detrimental consequences of social hierarchy or social isolation on welfare have been the main focus of a large portion of the research on social stress in animal models. Additionally, there is strong evidence that social rejection is a powerful trigger that triggers the stress response in humans (Dickerson and Kemeny, 2004). Our brains are more sensitive to signs of social exclusion because social membership was essential for survival in prehistoric cultures. The social environment actually engages with stress on nearly all levels: social interactions can be powerful stressors, they can act as a buffer against an external stressor, and stressful life events frequently cause social behaviour to shift. Examining the physiological and psychological impacts of virtual social environments is the next frontier in the relationship between stress and the social world, as these factors become more prominent in our everyday lives.

PSYCHOLOGICAL ASPECTS OF STRESS

Childhood and adolescent stressors include violence, abuse, and divorce/marital conflict. These can lead to psychological disorders, personality disorders, and poor school performance. Children of divorced parents often experience antisocial behavior, anxiety, and depression. War and terrorism exposure can result in PTSD and depressive symptoms in children. Chronic exposure to these stressors can lead to long-lasting neurobiological effects, increasing the risk of anxiety, mood disorders, aggressive decontrol problems, hypo-immune dysfunction, medical morbidity, structural changes in the CNS, and early death. These long-lasting effects can have long-lasting effects on an individual's mental health.

LIFE STRESS, ANXIETY, AND DEPRESSION

Stressful life events often lead to the onset of depression, as evidenced by studies in Denmark and cancer patients. Major negative life events, such as divorces, unemployment, and suicides, can also trigger depression. Long-term follow-up studies show that anxiety occurs more commonly before depression, and patients with anxiety are more likely to develop major depression after stressful life events occur.

DISORDERS RELATED TO TRAUMA

Traumatic events are highly prevalent in the general population, with estimates ranging from 40% to 70%. Acute Stress Disorder (ASD) and PTSD are two primary diagnoses related to trauma, with ASD lasting two days to four weeks and PTSD lasting one month. PTSD affects 1 in 12 adults at some time in their life. Trauma and disasters are related to concurrent depression, anxiety disorders, cognitive impairment, and substance abuse. Other consequences of stress, such as increases in smoking, substance use, accidents, sleep problems, and eating disorders, have been identified. Populations living in more stressful environments experience higher mortality rates from lung cancer and chronic obstructive pulmonary disorder. Life events stress and chronically stressful conditions have also been linked to higher consumption of alcohol, potentially using alcohol as self-medication for stress-related disorders. Increased sleep problems have been reported after psychological trauma, mediated by the new onset of sleep problems.

PSYCHOSOCIAL STRESSORS AND HEALTH

Psychosocial stressors have been linked to various diseases, including coronary heart disease (CHD), hypertension, and atherosclerosis. An occupational gradient in CHD risk is observed in men with low socioeconomic status, but this can be eliminated by addressing perceived job control and risky behaviors like smoking, alcohol use, and sedentary lifestyle. Work stress has been reported to be a predictor of incident CHD and hypertension in both men and women. However, marital stress is a better predictor of poor prognosis in women with existing CHD. Animal models, such as Kaplan et al.'s 1982 study on male cynomolgus monkeys, provide valuable insights into the specific influences of stressors on disease processes. The study found that socially dominant animals in unstable groups had more atherosclerosis than those in stable groups. Additionally, heart-rate reactivity to capture threat predicted the severity of atherosclerosis, and administrationoftheSNS-blockingagentpropranolol decreased atherosclerosis progression. McCabe et al.'s 2002 study found that affiliative social behavior can slow the progression of atherosclerosis in the Watanabe heritable hyperlipidemic rabbit model. Stress has been linked to exacerbations of autoimmune diseases and conditions with excessive inflammation, such as cardiovascular disease (CHD). This is due to a chronically activated, dysregulated acute stress response, which activates and migrates innate immune cells, mediated by proinflammatory cytokines. In healthy individuals, cortisol eventually suppresses proinflammatory cytokine production, but in autoimmune diseases or CHD, prolonged stress can cause chronic activation, exacerbating pathophysiology and symptoms. The glucocorticoid-resistance model suggests that immune cells become resistant to cortisol's effects, causing inflammation to continue indefinitely. This model could have implications for diseases of inflammation, such as rheumatoid arthritis, multiple sclerosis, and heart disease. Elevated levels of inflammatory markers, such as C-reactive protein, are predictive of heart attacks, even when controlling for other risk factors.

Inflammation, Cytokine Production, and Mental Health-

Prolonged proinflammatory cytokine production during illness can negatively impact mental health in vulnerable individuals. During times of illness, proinflammatory cytokines produce symptoms like fatigue, malaise, diminished appetite, and listlessness, which are usually associated with depression. These symptoms were once thought to be caused by infectious pathogens, but recent research shows that proinflammatory cytokines are necessary to generate sickness behavior. Sickness behavior is an adaptive response to illness stress, promoting resistance and recovery. However, it can become maladaptive when repeatedly activated. Elevated rates of depression are reported in patients with inflammatory diseases like MS and CHD, suggesting that stress contributes to both physical and mental disease through the mediating effects of proinflammatory cytokines.

HOST VULNERABILITY-STRESSOR INTERACTIONS AND DISEASE

Chronic stressors cause changes in biological set points across the lifespan, known as allostasis, and the biological cost of these adjustments is known as allostatic load. Cumulative increases in allostatic load are related to chronic illness, emphasizing the role of stressors in disease. However, the exact interactions between stressors, pathogens, host vulnerability, and poor health behaviors remain unclear. Changes in set points for variables like blood pressure may not be related to cumulative stressors, but they may play a role in multiple disease outcomes.

TREATMENT FOR STRESS-RELATED DISORDERS

Stress-related disorders like PTSD can be treated with cognitive-behavioral therapy (CBT), exposure, and Eye Movement Desensitization and Reprocessing. Psychopharmacological approaches and writing about trauma can also help. Beck's CBT and interpersonal therapy are effective for major depression patients. However, sleep problems or hypercortisolemia can hinder treatment. Combining psychotherapy and pharmacotherapy can be more effective for severe depression or recurrent depression. For anxiety, CBT and antidepressants can be effective, especially when GAD is comorbid with major depression. Psychosocial interventions, such as cognitive-behavioral stress management (CBSM), can improve the quality of life for patients with chronic diseases by decreasing perceived stress, improving social support, and promoting problem-focused coping.

Morbidity, Mortality, and Markers of Disease Progression-

Psychosocial intervention trials have shown both positive and null results in patients following acute myocardial infarction (MI). Two meta-analyses reported a reduction in mortality and morbidity of approximately 20% to 40%, with most studies conducted in men. The Recurrent Coronary Prevention Project (RCPP) employed group-based CBT, which decreased hostility and depressed affect and improved the composite medical end point of cardiac death and nonfatal MI. However, the Enhancing Recovery in Coronary Heart Disease (ENRICHD) clinical trial found modest decreases in depression and increased perceived social support but did not affect the composite medical end point of death and nonfatal MI. Future studies need to consider variables that may have prevented morbidity and mortality benefits among gender and ethnic subgroups other than white men.

Psychosocial intervention trials have also reported both positive and null results in patients with cancer. Some studies have significantly influenced factors associated with HIV/ AIDS disease progression, such as distress, depressed affect, denial coping, low perceived social support, and elevated serum cortisol. CBSM can positively influence stress-related variables associated with HIV/AIDS progression, but only a randomized clinical trial could document its specific decrease.

1.1 The Need for Stress Reduction: Importance of managing stress in modern life and the rise of stress-related health conditions.

Stress has emerged as a major issue that impacts almost every facet of daily living in the fast-paced world of today. Stress is a natural byproduct of the modern lifestyle, which includes social and personal difficulties as well as work-related demands. The prevalence of chronic stress in people of all ages and backgrounds has increased, making it critical to comprehend the significance of stress management. This chapter examines the importance of stress management, the effects of unmanaged stress on mental and physical health, and the increasing need for stress-reduction techniques in contemporary culture. Because stress-related health disorders are becoming more common in today's world, stress management has become more and more crucial. The repercussions of unmanaged stress may be both immediate and long-term, greatly affecting general health and well-being as life speeds up and people are continuously balancing social, career, and personal demands.

The Value of Stress Management

- *Mental Health:* Anxiety, depression, and burnout are just a few of the mental health conditions that are associated with prolonged stress. Emotional weariness, mood changes, impatience, and a sense of powerlessness can result from poorly managed stress.

- *Physical Health:* Stress causes the body to release hormones like cortisol and adrenaline, which trigger the "fight or flight" response. Short-term benefits may result from this, but prolonged activation of this response might impair immunity, damage the cardiovascular system, and interfere with sleep cycles. Conditions like heart disease, high blood pressure, and digestive problems may become more likely as a result.

- *Cognitive Functioning:* Concentration, memory, and decision-making are among the cognitive processes that stress adversely impact.

- *Relationships:* Both personal and professional relationships can be strained by stress. Stress can cause people to become more irritated, have trouble communicating, or retreat socially, which can strain relationships and make them feel alone.

- *Increase in Health Conditions Associated with Stress:* Stress-related health issues have alarmingly increased in recent years, reflecting the increasing demands people experience in today's society.

- *Cardiovascular Disease:* One of the main risk factors for heart disease and stroke is ongoing stress. Blood vessel damage and inflammation can result from the body's continuous secretion of stress hormones like cortisol and the elevated heart rate they induce. High stress levels have been linked to an increased risk of heart attacks and hypertension, according to studies.

- *Mental Health Disorders:* Over the past few decades, there has been a sharp increase in the prevalence of anxiety and depression. Chronic stress may have a significant role in these illnesses, according to research, especially when paired with environmental factors including job stress, social media pressure, and economic insecurity.

- *Autoimmune Diseases:* Prolonged stress can impair immunity and raise inflammation, increasing a person's risk of developing autoimmune conditions including lupus and rheumatoid arthritis. The body's own tissues may be attacked by an overactive immune system brought on by stress.

- *Digestive Issues:* The gastrointestinal system is known to be disturbed by stress. It may result in problems like acid reflux, ulcers, and irritable bowel syndrome (IBS). The digestive process slows down when the body is under stress, which causes discomfort and digestive distress.

- *sleep disorders:* One of the main causes of insomnia and other sleep disorders is stress. Stress hormones make it difficult to fall or stay asleep by interfering with the body's natural ability to relax. Stress is then made worse by inadequate sleep, starting a vicious cycle.

The Role of Modern Life in Stress

Modern life contributes to increased stress levels through workplace pressures, technological disruptions, social expectations, and economic stress. Workplace pressures, long hours, and blurred boundaries between work and home make it difficult to disconnect and recharge. Social media's unrealistic standards and rising living costs further exacerbate stress.

Strategies for Managing Stress

Managing stress is crucial for health, and effective strategies include mindfulness, meditation, exercise, sleep hygiene, time management, social support, and seeking professional help when overwhelmed. Mindfulness and meditation calm the mind, exercise releases endorphins, and prioritizes sleep. Time management strategies set boundaries, prioritize tasks, and take breaks. Engaging in meaningful social connections can provide emotional support and help reduce stress.

1.2 Using Medical Textiles to Reduce Stress

In a kingdom where mortals and gods coexisted, legendary healer Erya discovered that many people were overwhelmed by stress, clouding their minds and causing illnesses. Erya sought a solution that was practical and tied to the kingdom's ancient traditions. She traveled to the mystical mountains of Solvanta, where she met the Weaver Goddess, Aranya, who taught her the ancient art of creating textiles that can absorb and ease stress.

Aranya taught Erya the secret of using natural fibers from sacred trees, such as cotton spun from the Cottonwood Tree and silk from the Moon Moth. She also combined herbal dyes made from lavender, chamomile, and mint, known for their ability to promote relaxation.

Erya worked tirelessly, weaving garments and blankets imbued with these properties, which helped regulate the body's stress response, promoting relaxation, grounding, and balance. The people of the kingdom noticed a profound difference in their well-being, sleeping soundly, waking refreshed, and facing daily tasks with renewed energy and clarity.

Erya's work became renowned across the lands, and the gods took notice of her ability to intertwine the physical and spiritual worlds. They blessed her with eternal wisdom and named her the "Weaver of Calm." As the kingdom flourished, Erya's textiles were passed down through generations, becoming a symbol of peace and healing.It is becoming more widely acknowledged that stress, both mental and physical, is a serious health issue that can lead to anxiety, depression, heart problems, and other chronic illnesses. Medical textiles are a cutting-edge approach to stress management and reduction. Medical textiles have several important uses in stress treatment, such as:

Medical textiles, including compression garments, smart textiles, therapeutic textiles, and aromatherapy textiles, offer various benefits for physical and mental well-being. Compression garments enhance circulation and provide tactile pressure, reducing discomfort and anxiety. Smart textiles monitor physiological indicators, providing real-time data on stress levels. Therapeutic textiles, infused with essential oils or herbal extracts, provide soothing warmth for relaxation. Sleepwear and bedding designed for relaxation promote restful sleep. Aromatherapy textiles, infused with calming scents, can help reduce anxiety and stress.

Medical textiles are essential to contemporary healthcare because they help treat and manage a wide range of illnesses. Their uses cover new areas like stress management in addition to more established ones like wound care and surgical assistance. Medical textiles are assisting people in managing stress, enhancing mental health, and improving their general quality of life through advancements in compression therapy, smart textiles, and therapeutic materials. The use of cutting-edge textiles in healthcare procedures promises to significantly change how we think about mental and physical health as the sector develops.

Chapter 2:

The Science of Stress and Its Impact on Health-

In a kingdom where mortals and gods coexisted, legendary healer Erya discovered that many people were overwhelmed by stress, clouding their minds and causing illnesses. Erya sought a solution that was practical and tied to the kingdom's ancient traditions. She traveled to the mystical mountains of Solvanta, where she met the Weaver Goddess, Aranya, who taught her the ancient art of creating textiles that can absorb and ease stress.

Aranya taught Erya the secret of using natural fibers from sacred trees, such as cotton spun from the Cottonwood Tree and silk from the Moon Moth. She also combined herbal dyes made from lavender, chamomile, and mint, known for their ability to promote relaxation.

Erya worked tirelessly, weaving garments and blankets imbued with these properties, which helped regulate the body's stress response, promoting relaxation, grounding, and balance. The people of the kingdom noticed a profound difference in their well-being, sleeping soundly, waking refreshed, and facing daily tasks with renewed energy and clarity.

Erya's work became renowned across the lands, and the gods took notice of her ability to intertwine the physical and spiritual worlds. They blessed her with eternal wisdom and named her the "Weaver of Calm." As the kingdom flourished, Erya's textiles were passed down through generations, becoming a symbol of peace and healing.

2.1 The Role of the Nervous System in Stress: How stress affects the autonomic nervous system and the physiological changes it triggers. –

In Therra, a mystical land, the gods struggled to understand stress, a powerful force that affected mortals' nervous systems. Ithra, an ancient goddess of life's deepest mysteries, revealed that stress was not just a curse upon the soul but a powerful force that ravaged the nervous system of mortals. She explained that the sympathetic and parasympathetic nervous systems, together known as the autonomic nervous system, were responsible for the body's response to danger.

The sympathetic nervous system is quick to act when danger arises, sending signals that prepare the body for action. However, when danger is no longer present, the body remains on high alert. The parasympathetic nervous system, the healer of the body, restores balance by slowing the heart, easing the breath, and relaxing the muscles. When stress is prolonged, the sympathetic system never truly shuts down, leading to physiological changes that wear down the body and mind.

Ithra explained that when the sympathetic nervous system is triggered, it must be countered with the calm of the parasympathetic system. Mortals must learn to find ways to return to peace, slow the rush of adrenaline and cortisol, and to return to rest. Ancient practices that could restore balance between the two systems include breathing exercises, mindfulness and meditation, physical movement, nature's healing power, and sleep and rest.

With this knowledge, Aetheron returned to Therra and shared the wisdom of the gods with the mortals of Therra. They learned how to listen to their bodies and calm their nervous systems, slowly finding peace. The story of how the gods revealed the mysteries of the nervous system and the physiological impacts of stress became a legend passed down through generations, reminding people that while stress was a part of life, balance was always within reach, and with the right tools, they could restore peace to their minds, bodies, and spirits.Stress triggers a complex network of physiological systems, especially the autonomic nervous system (ANS), and is the body's normal reaction to perceived threats or challenges. The ANS is essential for controlling involuntary body processes that are affected by stress, including blood pressure, respiration, digestion, and heart rate. Recognizing the ways stress impacts both physical and mental health requires an understanding of how stress impacts the ANS.

The Autonomic Nervous System (ANS) Overview

There are three primary parts to the autonomic nervous system:

- Often called the "fight or flight" system, the sympathetic nervous system (SNS) is triggered in reaction to stress. By raising heart rate, widening pupils, and rerouting blood flow to muscles, it primes the body to react to danger.

- Often referred to as the "rest and digest" system, the parasympathetic nervous system (PNS) helps the body relax following a stress reaction. After the body's fight-or-flight reaction has been triggered, it decreases heart rate, aids in digestion, and speeds up recuperation.

The sympathetic and parasympathetic branches of the nervous system regulate the enteric nervous system (ENS), sometimes referred to as the "second brain," which controls the operations of the gastrointestinal tract. The sympathetic and parasympathetic nervous systems are out of balance when stress arises, which causes a number of physiological alterations meant to prime the body for quick action.

2.2 Sympathetic Nervous System (SNS) Activation

Stress sets off what is usually referred to as the "fight or flight" response, which activates the SNS. The hypothalamus receives a signal from the brain when it detects a stressor, and the sympathetic nervous system is triggered. Stress chemicals including noradrenaline (norepinephrine) and adrenaline (epinephrine) are released as a result. These hormones cause the body to undergo a number of changes, such as:

Elevated blood pressure and heart rate: The body is primed for action as the heart beats more quickly to pump more oxygen and nutrients to the muscles and essential organs.

- **Pupil dilation:** This enhances vision and environmental awareness by letting more light into the eyes.

- **Increased respiration rate:** To meet the body's increased physical needs, the lungs take in more oxygen.

- **Redirected blood flow:** To prepare the body for quick activity, blood vessels widen in muscles and constrict in non-essential organs (such as the digestive system).

- **Fatty acid and glucose release:** The liver mobilizes fatty acids for long-term energy requirements and releases glucose to give muscles a rapid energy source.

In brief bursts, these adaptations aid the body's rapid reaction to danger. On the other hand, long-term or chronic stress keeps the SNS active, which might have negative health repercussions.

The Autonomic Domain, a kingdom in the human body, was ruled by two deities: Sympathos, the God of Alertness and Action, and Parasympus, the God of Calm and Rest. Together, they maintained balance and ensured the body could both fight and find peace. When the Terror of the Unknown threatened the kingdom, Sympathos summoned the SNS, a network of messengers and warriors, to prepare the body for battle. The body's adrenal glands released adrenaline, amplifying energy and readiness. The eyes glowed with heightened awareness, pupils dilated, and lungs expanded to maintain strength. The SNS sent messengers to the muscles, preparing them for battle. Parasympus, the God of Calm and Rest, intervened to restore balance and remind the body that not every challenge requires violence. Sympathos summoned noradrenaline, sharpening the mind and body for the fight. The Terror of the Unknown was defeated, and peace returned. The balance between Sympathos and Parasympus reflects how the SNS and Parasympathetic Nervous System work together to maintain the body's equilibrium, heightening alertness in times of need and ensuring rest and calm once danger has passed.

2.3 The Hypothalamic-Pituitary-Adrenal (HPA) Axis is activated.

Stress also triggers the HPA axis, which includes the pituitary, adrenal, and hypothalamus, in addition to the SNS. By generating cortisol, the main stress hormone, this system contributes significantly to the body's reaction to stress. This is how the HPA axis functions:

The pituitary gland releases adrenocorticotropic hormone (ACTH) in response to stimulation from the hypothalamus' release of corticotropin-releasing hormone (CRH).

1. Cortisol is released when ACTH reaches the adrenal glands.

2. By boosting glucose availability for energy, inhibiting non-essential processes (such as the immunological response), and preserving cardiovascular stability under stress, cortisol aids the body in managing stress.

3. Although cortisol is essential for managing stress in the short term, persistently high cortisol levels can have detrimental effects on health, such as:

   ○ Reduced ability to fight

   ○ Elevated blood pressure

   ○ Gaining weight, particularly belly fat

   ○ Depression and anxiety

- Memory and cognitive function impairment

4. Stress Recuperation and the Parasympathetic Nervous System (PNS)

The parasympathetic nervous system takes over to return the body to its normal, non-stressed state when the threat has been eliminated or the stressor has disappeared. The "rest and digest" phase is the term for this process. It encourages rest and recuperation while counteracting the effects of the SNS.

During parasympathetic activity, important alterations include

Reduced blood pressure and heart rate: The blood pressure and heart rate both drop back to normal.

Improved immunological response and digestion: Blood flow is diverted to the digestive organs, facilitating the absorption of nutrients and the healing process.

Decreased respiratory rate: Deeper and slower breathing.

Muscle relaxation: Tension in the muscles that was increased during stress starts to lessen.

Chronic stress might hinder the body's capacity to properly activate the PNS, but the parasympathetic system's capacity to "calm the body" is crucial for post-stress recovery. This can lead to a dysregulated stress response, in which the body is unable to return to a state of rest because it is always in a state of heightened alertness.

2.4 Chronic Stress and Its Effects on the Nervous System

Prolonged stress over activates the ANS and HPA axis, resulting in physiological alterations like tense muscles, reduced immune systems, digestive troubles, cardiovascular problems, and mental health disorders. Burnout, ulcers, acid reflux, irritable bowel syndrome, high blood pressure, and an elevated heart rate can all be caused by these problems.

6. Balancing the Nervous System: Strategies for Stress Management

Finding strategies to trigger the parasympathetic nervous system and bring the body back to a calm state is essential for managing the effects of stress on the nervous system. Strategies that work include:

Relaxation techniques: Activities that help activate the PNS and lessen the effects of stress on the body include deep breathing, meditation, and mindfulness.

Physical activity: Exercise encourages the release of endorphins, the body's natural mood enhancers, and lowers the production of stress hormones.

Getting enough sleep is crucial for recovering from stress. It enables the body to regain equilibrium and aids in cortisol regulation.

Bodywork and massage: These methods can help to stimulate the parasympathetic nervous system by promoting relaxation and releasing tense muscles.

3 . The Role of Textiles in Healthcare

Surgical drapes are crucial tools for maintaining sterility and preventing the spread of infections during a range of surgical procedures. They intend to reduce the risk of contamination by erecting a physical barrier between the surgical site and the surroundings.

These specially designed sheets are intended to act as a sterile barrier between the surgery site and the surrounding environment. They are composed of nonwoven fabric, which is impervious to liquids and microbes. Drapes assist lower the risk of infection and the spread of pollutants during surgery by keeping the operating area distinct.

Surgical drapes are used in hospitals for various purposes. Disposable drapes are single-use, sterile, and convenient for specific body areas. Reusable drapes are cost-effective, eco-friendly, and can be cleaned and sanitized multiple times. Unique drapes are designed for specific medical specialties, such as obstetrics/gynaecology or neurology, providing unique solutions for specific surgical needs. Patient safety drapes are designed to enhance safety during surgery by preventing unintentional harm like electrical burns. They are essential for electrosurgical operations and laparoscopic procedures. Impervious drapes, made from materials that prevent fluid flow, are used in orthopaedic or irrigation surgeries to maintain cleanliness in the surgical field.

3.1 Care for wounds

Various fabric manufacturing processes, including knitting, weaving, braiding, crocheting, composite materials, and non-woven technologies, are employed in modern wound care.[46] Materials and products with noticeably better qualities made using cutting-edge technology and innovative techniques are research topics in medical textiles. An developing industry with substantial growth in wound care products is new medical textiles. All of these qualities are crucial for wound care fibres and dressings. They are haemostatic, absorbent, biocompatible, breathable, non-toxic, and non-allergic. They have good mechanical qualities as well. Products made from chitosan, alginate, collagen, branan ferulate, and carbon fibre have many benefits over traditional materials. Foams, hydrogels, films, hydrocolloids, and matrix (tissue engineering) are additional materials utilised in wound treatment.

Compression Clothing

Specially made textiles known as compression garments are used to provide regulated pressure to certain body areas. In medical contexts, these clothes are frequently used to promote circulation, lessen oedema, and aid in recovery. They are frequently recommended for individuals recuperating from surgery, treating long-term illnesses, or enhancing the functionality of particular body parts.

Compression garment types include:

> **Elastic Bandages:** Injured limbs or places that are prone to swelling are frequently wrapped with traditional bandages, such the well-known "ACE bandage." The afflicted area is evenly compressed by these bandages.

> **The process of compression:** Generally speaking, stockings and socks are used to increase blood flow and decrease swelling, especially in individuals who have venous disorders, oedema, or have had surgery. They come in three different pressure levels: mild, moderate, and strong.

> **Post-operative Garments:** Following surgery (such as orthopedic, breast, or liposuction), compression garments serve to support the operative site, minimise oedema, and avoid fluid buildup.

> **Therapeutic Garments for Lymphoedema:** Patients with lymphoedema, a disorder in which fluid builds up in the tissues, are treated with specialized compression garments. These clothes aid in the drainage of fluids and stop further swelling.

Compression garments' purposes include:

- **Improved Circulation:** By encouraging venous return, compression garments lessen fluid retention and swelling while also enhancing blood circulation.

- **Support for Soft Tissues:** By offering extra support, they aid in stabilizing muscles and joints, especially following operations or accidents.

- **Prevention of Deep Vein Thrombosis (DVT):** In order to stop blood clots from forming in patients who are bedridden or immobilized, compression stockings are frequently advised.

Compression garments are frequently used in medicine.

- **Sports Injuries:** By lowering swelling and supporting injured muscles, compression garments can lower the chance of injury and speed up healing.

- **Post-Surgery Recovery:** Compression garments aid in body contouring and post-operative oedema reduction following procedures such as breast augmentation or liposuction.

- **Chronic Venous Insufficiency:** To lessen pain and swelling, individuals with varicose veins or chronic venous insufficiency are frequently recommended compression stockings.

For many years, traditional medical textiles such as compression garments, surgical drapes, and wound care items have been vital to the healthcare industry. By promoting healing, avoiding infections, and increasing comfort, these fabrics have played a crucial role in improving patient outcomes. Better support, protection, and utility are all made possible by the ongoing development of increasingly sophisticated, specialized textiles. These conventional applications will keep changing as technology advances, introducing fresh materials and methods to further enhance patient comfort and care.

3.2 Innovative Applications in Stress Relief: Textiles Designed for Stress Management, Relaxation, and Comfort

Innovative solutions created especially for stress alleviation and general well-being have been added to the field of medical textiles in recent years, expanding beyond their usual use. In today's world, stress—both psychological and physical—is a major worry, which is why there is a growing need for fabrics that encourage comfort, relaxation, and stress relief. These cutting-edge textiles use cutting-edge materials, patterns, and technology to enhance health and reduce stress. Some of the most well-known uses of textiles intended to reduce stress are listed below:

Stress-Relieving Compression Textiles

Compression garments are intended to reduce tension and anxiety in addition to their medical uses, which include enhancing circulation and offering post-operative support. Applying controlled pressure to particular body regions can assist relax the nervous system and provide a sensation of peace, according to the theory underlying compression treatment for stress management.

Compression Textile Types for Stress Reduction:

- *Compression vests:* These devices deliver mild pressure to the torso, which can soothe the nervous system and are frequently used for people with anxiety or sensory processing issues. The reassuring experience of being embraced is said to be replicated by this "hugging" sensation.

- *Gloves or compression sleeves:* These items of clothing apply specific pressure.

In order to prolong the advantages of aromatherapy throughout the day, textiles are now being infused with essential oils or smells. Aromatherapy has long been used to encourage relaxation and lower stress levels.

Textile Types for Aromatherapy:

Aromatherapy Pillows & Cushions: Especially when used for meditation or sleep, pillows made of materials that emit calming aromas like eucalyptus, lavender, or chamomile can help people relax and feel less stressed.

- *Sleepwear with a scent:* Some sleepwear is infused with essential oils, which gradually release their scent. These clothes could be nightgowns, sleep masks, or bed sheets with relaxing fragrances that encourage deeper, more peaceful slumber.

- *Embedded Bedding with Aromatherapy:* Blankets or bed linens composed of fibers infused with essential oils can assist create a peaceful sleeping environment, promoting a deeper sleep, which is essential for stress reduction.

Therapeutic Heat or Cooling Integrated into Textiles

Because temperature has a direct impact on comfort and relaxation, it is a critical component of stress management. More and more people are using textiles with heating or cooling properties to help them relax and reduce stress.

Types of Textiles with Therapeutic Temperature Regulation:

- *Heated Clothes:* Clothes and accessories like heated jackets, blankets, or wraps can offer calming warmth to ease tense muscles, increase blood flow, and produce a cosy atmosphere that reduces stress.

- *Cooling Clothing:* In stressful circumstances, such as when someone is overheated from anxiety or physical activity, clothing made to absorb and distribute heat is worn to help reduce body temperature. Cooling materials are frequently used in clothing items such as wristbands, caps, and vests.

Intelligent Textiles with Stress Monitoring and Biofeedback

The use of biofeedback in textiles has created new opportunities for real-time stress management as wearable technology has grown in popularity. Sensor-enabled smart textiles can track physiological indicators of stress, including skin temperature, breathing, and heart rate, and either provide feedback or initiate therapeutic reactions.

Smart Textile Types for Stress Reduction:

Smart shirts, vests, or wristbands that track heart rate variability and notify the wearer when stress levels increase are known as heart rate monitoring wearables. These clothes frequently connect to smartphone apps that provide deep breathing techniques and guided meditation, among other relaxation techniques.

Textiles that stimulate the neurological system with tiny electrical pulses or vibrations in order to lessen tension or anxiety are known as neurostimulation garments.

Textiles with Weights for Intense Pressure Stimulation

In recent years, weighted textiles—like weighted blankets—have become more and more popular due to their capacity to induce deep pressure stimulation, which promotes relaxation and lowers stress. The idea behind this type of therapy is that deep touch pressure (DPT) can trigger the parasympathetic nervous system, which lowers cortisol levels and fosters calm.

Weighted textile types include:

- *Weighted Blankets:* These blankets apply a mild, uniform pressure to the body since they are packed with materials like glass beads or plastic pellets. It has been demonstrated that the weight improves relaxation and the quality of sleep by producing an embrace-like sensation.

- *Weighted Vest:* These vests put pressure on the wearer's torso to help reduce anxiety.

Textiles for Mindfulness and Meditation

Another creative method to use fabrics for stress treatment is through materials made especially to support mindfulness or meditation techniques. These textiles can help create a peaceful atmosphere that promotes concentration, deep relaxation, and stress reduction.

Types of Textiles for Mindfulness and Meditation:

- *Meditation mats and cushions:* specially crafted mats or cushions composed of natural materials (such as wool or cotton) that support comfortable posture and encourage focus and relaxation during meditation.

Wearables that stimulate the senses through touch or vibration are known as mindfulness wearables, and they help people stay focused and grounded when practicing mindfulness.

3.3 Bioactive Fabrics: Introduction to fabrics that release active agents such as scents, heat, or vibration to reduce stress.

Bacterial contamination of textile fabric surfaces is a common hazard in the medical healthcare sector, and the COVID-19 pandemic has highlighted the need for eco-friendly antimicrobial materials. Cotton fabrics are commonly used for medical and biomedical purposes, but they have poor resistance against microbial growth, limiting their use in advanced medical applications. Several approaches have been proposed to improve the antibacterial properties of cotton-based materials, including chemical coatings, stabilization of metal nanoparticles, and surface plasma treatment. However, traditional chemical additives are often non-biodegradable, causing environmental pollution and affecting human health.

Chitosan biopolymer coatings offer a promising alternative due to their unique properties, including biodegradability, biocompatibility, film-forming capacity, non-toxicity, and antimicrobial activity. Combining chitosan coating with functional eco-friendly additives could add further benefits, such as antibacterial, antifungal, biodegradable, and safe for human health properties. Several studies have shown that chitosan/herbal composites can create antimicrobial cotton fabrics, with good antibacterial activity observed for other cotton fabrics modified with different plant extracts. However, there have been no significant studies on antimicrobial cotton fabrics modified with chitosan coatings containing both plant extracts and essential oils. This study presents bioactive and biodegradable cotton fabrics designed for single-use medical textile applications, focusing on the effects of functionalization with chitosan-based coatings on structure, color, thermal stability, biodegradability, and anti-microbial activity. This eco-friendly approach paves the way for developing antibacterial coating systems for cotton fabrics, with potential applications in various medical sectors.

An inventive and new type of textiles known as "bioactive fabrics" is designed to release active ingredients like heat, vibration, or fragrances in order to encourage relaxation, lower stress levels, and improve overall health. These textiles offer a dynamic and proactive approach to stress management by utilising the inherent or designed qualities of materials to immediately apply therapeutic benefits through skin contact. Incorporating bioactive components into textiles is a promising development in the fields of consumer health and medicine, providing fresh approaches to stress reduction in daily life.

Textiles that are made to interact with the environment and human body in ways that can improve health and well-being are known as bioactive fabrics. These textiles are designed to deliver active agents using integrated or embedded systems, including:

Fragrances or essential oils that are gradually released to have a relaxing effect are known as aromatherapy scents.

> *Heat:* Textiles with the ability to produce or hold heat are used to relax the body and ease tense muscles.

> *Vibrations:* Textiles that use mild vibrations to ease stress and encourage rest.

Advanced textile engineering is usually used to manufacture these fabrics, which include materials that can be activated under particular conditions (e.g., time, temperature, or pressure). Bioactive textiles offer a novel approach to treating mental health issues such as stress, anxiety, and harnessing the body's innate reactions to stimuli to treat insomnia.

Bioactive Fabric Types for Stress Reduction: a. Fabrics Infused with Aromatherapy The capacity of aromatherapy to reduce stress and elevate mood is well known. Essential oils or smells that are released gradually over time can be integrated into bioactive fabrics to create a relaxing effect that lasts all day. Known for their calming qualities, eucalyptus, lavender, and chamomile are frequently used fragrances in aromatherapy textiles.

- *How It Works:* To retain and release smells, aromatherapy fabrics frequently employ microencapsulation processes. When the fabric comes into contact with the skin, friction or body heat activates the aroma. After that, the scent is gradually released, which aids in lowering tension, calming anxiety, and encouraging deeper sleep.

- *Applications:* Textiles that use fragrances to aid include therapeutic cushions, blankets, sheets, sleepwear, and aromatherapy pillows.

  b. *Textiles That Produce Heat:* A tried-and-true technique for easing physical stress and encouraging relaxation is heat treatment. The ability of bioactive textiles to produce or hold heat can assist relax tense muscles, lessen discomfort, and promote relaxation.

- *How It Operates:* Phase change materials (PCMs) and conductive fibres, which store heat and release it gradually, are frequently used in these textiles. Certain textiles, such battery-operated heated blankets or clothing, may be made to warm up in response to body heat or a linked power source.

- *Applications:* Compresses, heated blankets, wraps, and therapeutic apparel are among the goods made from heat treatment textiles. These materials can ease discomfort, ease tense muscles, and encourage relaxation, particularly in people who have tight muscles from stress.

c. Textiles that Can Vibrate Vibration therapy can help reduce tension, increase circulation, and encourage relaxation by stimulating the skin and muscles with mild oscillations or movements. Vibration technology in bioactive textiles is intended to give the wearer a mild, calming massage.

- *How It Operates:* When actuated, these fabrics' tiny vibrational motors or actuators produce pulsed or rhythmic vibrations. The frequency and strength of the vibrations can be changed to create a personalized relaxation experience.

- *Applications:* By providing a relaxing massage, wearable vibration therapy textiles, such as vests, shirts, or wraps, can help ease tension and reduce stress. These fabrics can help with muscular relaxation, stress reduction, and better sleep.

Bioactive fabrics provide controlled sensory input that interacts with the body's natural stress response mechanisms. Agents like aromatherapy, heat therapy, and vibration stimulate physiological processes for relaxation and stress relief. Aromatherapy affects the limbic system, lowering heart rate and blood pressure, and triggering the release of endorphins. Heat therapy promotes vasodilation, pain relief, and relaxation, while vibration therapy stimulates proprioceptors, enhancing circulation and reducing stress-induced muscle tension.

4. Materials and Technologies Used in Stress-Reducing Medical Textiles

Thermal conditions are crucial for human health and productivity, and personal thermal management focusing on thermal conditions is emerging as an energy-efficient and cost-effective solution. Innovative textiles have been designed to control human body heat dissipation routes, such as radiation, convection, conduction, and evaporation. However, for intense scenarios, textiles for ideal personal perspiration or evaporation management are still lacking.

Evaporation plays an indispensable role in human body thermoregulation, with 20% of heat dissipation of the dry human body relying on water vapor loss via insensible perspiration. State-of-the-art textiles for daily use are usually sufficient at water vapor transmission to ensure comfort at the mild state. However, the cooling performance of conventional textiles needs improvement when the human body is in more intense scenarios, such as moderate/profuse perspiration situations.

Sweat removal is essential for human body thermoregulation, but conventional textiles have limited evaporative cooling efficiency due to limited heat transfer from the skin. This results in increased wettedness on the skin and decreased evaporative cooling efficiency. Inefficient cooling can lead to further perspiration and accumulation of sweat in the textile, which can undermine the buffer effect of the textiles once the absorption limit is reached.

In this work, a novel concept of integrated cooling (i-Cool) textile is proposed, which integrates heat conductive components into the textile and divides the functionalities of heat conduction and sweat transport into two operational components. The i-Cool textile functions not only to wick sweat but also provides heat conduction paths for accelerated evaporation and efficiently takes away a great amount of heat from the skin. The enhanced evaporation ability and high sweat evaporative cooling efficiency can prevent the i-Cool textile from flooding and avoiding excessive perspiration.

4.1 Textiles with moisture-wicking and breathable properties

Breathable fabric allows air to pass through it, helping to regulate body temperature and prevent moisture buildup. When you understand the microscopic structure of such fabrics, it's easier to see how they achieve these benefits.

These fabrics are designed with tiny pores or gaps that permit **airflow**, a fundamental aspect engineered meticulously by **textile engineers**. In textile engineering, creating **breathable fabric** involves balancing the size and distribution of these pores. If the pores are too large, the fabric loses its durability and structure. If they're too small, air can't pass through effectively.

For a number of uses, such as stress-relieving clothing, sportswear, and medical textiles, moisture-wicking and breathable textiles are essential. These textiles' special qualities aid in controlling temperature, controlling moisture, and boosting comfort—all of which can lessen stress or promote general wellbeing. A closer examination of these textile qualities is provided below:

1. Moisture-wicking textiles are designed to pull moisture away from the body, allowing it to evaporate. They are commonly used in sportswear, activewear, medical textiles, and stress-reducing garments. These fabrics work through capillary action, drawing moisture away from the skin and evaporating once it reaches the fabric's surface. Synthetic fibers like polyester, nylon, and acrylic are commonly used.

2. Breathable textiles allow air to circulate through the fabric, promoting ventilation and temperature regulation. They are made from natural fibers like cotton, linen, and merino wool, synthetic fibers like polyester or nylon, and membrane fabrics like Gore-Tex. They are used in athletic and medical clothing, hospital gowns, compression garments, and

post-surgery clothing to promote air circulation and prevent conditions like pressure ulcers. Breathable fabrics also enhance comfort during meditation, yoga, or sleep.

3. Moisture-wicking and breathable properties in textiles enhance comfort and stress reduction. They draw sweat away from the skin, while the breathable fabric circulates air, facilitating moisture evaporation and heat dissipation. This balance ensures a comfortable, dry, and cool environment. Applications include compression garments, sleepwear, and therapeutic clothing for stress-relieving therapies and conditions like restless leg syndrome or anxiety.

4. Moisture-wicking and breathable textiles offer numerous benefits for stress reduction, including comfort, improved sleep quality, physical relaxation, and reduced skin irritation. Future trends include smart textiles with sensors for real-time moisture adjustments, sustainable materials using organic fibers, and advanced activewear and wearables that combine moisture-wicking and breathable properties with other technologies. These advancements are crucial for managing stress and promoting healthier lifestyles.

4.2 Anti-microbial and hypoallergenic textiles-

Particularly for people with sensitive skin or allergies, antimicrobial and hypoallergenic materials are made especially to enhance cleanliness, lessen discomfort, and guarantee comfort. These textiles are designed or treated to fulfil particular purposes that improve their comfort, safety, and health. Suitable for people with sensitive skin or those who are prone to allergies, antimicrobial and hypoallergenic textiles are made to provide protection against dangerous microorganisms (such as bacteria, fungi, and viruses) and to reduce allergic reactions. These textiles are frequently utilized in many different purposes, including upholstery, medical materials, beds, and clothes.

Textiles that are anti-bacterial:

The goal of treating these textiles with antimicrobial chemicals is to stop bacteria, fungi, and other microorganisms from growing and spreading since they can lead to odour, infection, or fabric deterioration.

Techniques of Production:

- **Chemical treatments:** antibacterial compounds with inherent antibacterial qualities, such as copper, zinc, or silver ions, are used to treat some fabrics.

- **Natural fibers:** Because of their structure and capacity to drain away moisture, some natural fibers, such as wool and silk, naturally possess antibacterial qualities.

- **Nanotechnology:** To achieve long-lasting antibacterial benefits, several fabrics include nano-silver or other nanoparticles.

Common uses include bed linens, medical uniforms, socks, underwear, and sportswear.

Allergy-reducing textiles:

The goal of hypoallergenic textiles is to lessen the possibility of allergic reactions. Using materials that are less prone to irritate skin or trigger allergic reactions helps achieve this.

Important Features:

- *Breathability:* A lot of hypoallergenic materials are breathable, which permits airflow and avoids moisture accumulation that can aggravate skin irritation or encourage the growth of dust mites and other allergens.

- *Natural fibers:* Because they are softer and less likely to irritate skin, fabrics made from natural fibers like cotton, bamboo, or organic linen are frequently hypoallergenic.

- *Low Chemical Content:* Synthetic treatments, chemicals, and dyes that can trigger allergies are typically absent from hypoallergenic textiles.

- *Finishing treatments:* Eco-friendly anti-irritant finishes or enzyme washes are examples of natural anti-allergy treatments applied to certain textiles. Common Uses: Clothes, bedding, mattresses, and towels made for those with dermatitis, eczema, or asthma who have sensitive skin.

Examples of Anti-microbial and Hypoallergenic Textiles:

Bamboo fabric, silver-infused fabrics, tencel/lyocell, organic cotton, and Merino wool are all hypoallergenic textiles. Bamboo fibers are naturally antimicrobial, breathable, and moisture-wicking, while silver-infused fabrics have antibacterial properties. Organic cotton is gentle on the skin and free of harsh chemicals.

Applications: -

Anti-microbial and hypoallergenic fabrics are essential in healthcare, sportswear, and home textiles for preventing infections, controlling odor, and providing a healthier sleep environment.

Maintenance: -

Anti-microbial textiles require multiple washes, while hypoallergenic textiles require gentler detergents or washing methods to avoid irritation.

4.3 Smart textile and wearables –

Feedback system that promotes relaxation – A smart textiles and wearables feedback system can provide real-time data and interactions to help individuals manage stress and promote calmness.

1. **Sensors and Data Collection:** Smart textiles and wearables use biometric sensors to monitor physiological

parameters, such as heart rate, skin temperature, respiration rate, and sweat levels, to detect stress and relaxation levels, and brainwave activity.

2. **Real-time Feedback:** Auditory Feedback (Sound Therapy): Using built-in speakers or bone conduction technology, the wearable might play relaxing music or noises based on the data gathered. You can adjust the sound frequencies (e.g., natural noises, binaural beats) to encourage relaxation.

3. **Vibration Feedback:** The wearable can offer haptic feedback, such as rhythmic pulsing that simulates deep breathing patterns or a light massage, or soothing vibrations that are intended to relax the body.

4. **Visual Feedback (Light Therapy):** LEDs or smart textiles that change colour in response to the wearer's stress levels can be integrated into smart textiles. When someone is under stress, soothing hues like blue or green may be triggered, which would help create a visual cue to calm down.

5. **Exercises for Relaxation and Guided Breathing:**

6. **Guided Breathing Prompts:** The wearable could lead the user through breathing workouts using haptic or audible feedback. For example, it might ask the user to take a deep breath for four counts, hold it for four counts, and then release it for four counts. A relaxed state and

a lowered heart rate can result from this controlled breathing.

7. **Progressive Muscle Relaxation (PMR):** To promote physical relaxation, the system may ask the user to tense and relax various muscle groups. The user can be guided through this process with haptic feedback.

8. **Data Visualisation and Tracking:** Integration with Mobile Apps: A mobile app that monitors advancement over time can be linked to the wearable gadget. In order to help users understand their relaxation patterns and pinpoint triggers, the app might display visual representations of stress levels, heart rate variability, and other information.

9. **Biofeedback:** Users can learn to regulate their stress reaction by seeing real-time data. With the help of biofeedback, the wearable can instruct users on how to modify their posture and breathing patterns in order to achieve a relaxed state.

10. **Examples of Wearable Technology:**

11. **Smart Clothing:** Sensor-equipped clothing may continuously track the wearer's physiological signals and provide feedback by vibrating or displaying patterns of light on the fabric.

12. **Smart Jewelry:** Sensors on wearable bracelets or rings can identify changes in the body and give haptic feedback. They can also link to a smartphone app for coaching in relaxing.

13. **Headbands or Earwear:** Wearables that can identify heart rate or brainwave activity, such as headbands or earbuds, can then lead the user in mindfulness exercises, deep breathing, or meditation.

14. **Personalized Relaxation:** Adaptive Systems: The system can identify the user's particular stressors and preferences by using the data collected. The feedback mechanisms (music, vibration, light, etc.) might be changed over time to see what works best for the user.

15. **Environment-aware Relaxation:** To maximise relaxation in various contexts (e.g., a noisy office versus a quiet home), the wearable might additionally adjust its feedback systems to take into account environmental factors like temperature, light exposure, and noise levels.

Example of wearable stress reducing textile –

Examples of wearable stress-reduction tools that can ease tension and encourage relaxation include the following:

1. **Muse Headband**

   By giving users real-time feedback on their brain activity, the Muse is a brain-sensing headband that facilitates meditation. It helps lower stress and increase mindfulness by using EEG (electroencephalography) sensors to track brain waves and providing audio cues to direct attention and relaxation.

2. Spire Stone

Spire is a wearable gadget that monitors your breathing patterns and fastens to your clothes. It tracks your breathing to identify stress indicators and gently reminds you to relax and take deep breaths when you're feeling particularly tense.

3. Tracker of Pip Stress

The Pip is a portable gadget that tracks skin conductivity to determine stress levels. It functions by giving users biofeedback as they engage in particular activities, such breathing techniques, which promote relaxation and reduce stress.

4. Heart Math Inner Balance

Attached to your ear, this gadget is a sensor that links to a smartphone app. It provides real-time input to assist control emotions and evaluates heart rate variability (HRV). Users can lessen stress and enhance their emotional health by engaging in breathing exercises.

5. **Feelings**

A wearable gadget called Feel mind was created to enhance emotional equilibrium. It tracks physiological indicators of stress and anxiety using biofeedback, and then offers treatments (such deep breathing techniques) to help people relax again.

6. **The Ring of Oura**

The Oura Ring is a smart ring that monitors a number of parameters, such as heart rate variability, exercise, and sleep quality. By examining trends linked to both physical and mental health, it offers insights into general stress levels, assisting users in managing stress and maximising their recuperation.

7. A sleep mask called Neuron has sensors integrated within it to track vital signs, sleep cycles, and brain activity. By offering sleep insights and encouraging relaxing strategies to enhance sleep quality and mental clarity, it assists users in managing stress.

8. **Cooling Pill**

A little, portable gadget that helps you relax when you're stressed by combining biofeedback and deep breathing techniques. It encourages relaxation by softly vibrating while you follow slow, steady breathing techniques.

5. evidence and research on stress reducing textile

5.1 overview of students on the efficiency of stress reducing textiles-

1. clinical studies and trials –

A summary of student research on the effectiveness of stress-relieving textiles frequently concentrates on the ways in which particular textiles or styles of clothing might lessen the negative effects of stress on the body and mind. This expanding field of study looks at how textiles—such as compression clothing, therapeutic fabrics, and clothing made for sensory stimulation—affect comfort, stress reduction, and general well-being. The following are some main ideas that are frequently covered in student studies on this subject:

1. Healing Textiles

2. Socks, tights, and sleeves are examples of compression clothing. These items are made to exert constant pressure on the body, which can increase blood flow and have a relaxing effect. Research frequently focusses on the ways in which these clothes enhance posture, encourage relaxation, and lessen anxiety.

3. *Weighted Textiles:* Like weighted blankets, certain clothing items are made to stimulate deep pressure touch, which lowers stress by causing the brain's dopamine and

serotonin levels to rise. They are well-liked by those with anxiety or sensory processing problems because of the comfort and reassurance that this tactile stimulation can provide.

4. Using Fabric Technology to Reduce Stress

5. Smart textiles are made with sensors or conductive fibres that can track a number of physiological variables, including skin conductivity, temperature, and heart rate. Additionally, certain smart textiles can provide biofeedback or micro-vibrations to the wearer's skin to assist them become more conscious of their stress levels and learn how to control them.

6. Using aromatherapy in textiles: Some textiles have scented compounds or essential oils embedded into them, which gradually release soothing scents. Studies in this field could look at how wearing these materials affects stress levels and mood throughout the day.

7. Advantages for the Physiology and Psychology

8. *Decrease in Stress and Anxiety:* A lot of student research focusses on how wearing textiles that reduce stress lowers cortisol levels, a hormone linked to stress, and encourages relaxation. Students who wear these clothes may experience less anxiety and feel more at ease in stressful situations like work or school.

9. *Better Sleep Quality:* According to some study, using specific textiles—like weighted blankets or clothing with relaxing properties—may assist enhance sleep quality by encouraging relaxation and lowering stress or anxiety at night.

10. Student-Focused Applications

Students with Exam Stress: A common focus of student research is the use of stress-reducing textiles in educational settings. Stress from exams and deadlines can be mitigated through the use of certain textiles, such as weighted vests or calming garments, to help students maintain composure and focus during high-stress periods.

Support for Mental Health: Research often emphasizes how stress-reducing textiles could be incorporated into daily life for students who experience anxiety, depression, or stress, offering a non-pharmaceutical intervention for mental health management.

5.2 .Environmental and Design Considerations-

Stress-reducing textiles can be beneficial for mental health and the environment, as they incorporate sustainable materials. The aesthetic appeal of these garments also influences their effectiveness. However, there is limited research on long-term effects, individual variability, and cost and accessibility challenges. Long-term effects may be limited due to personal preferences and body types, while cost can limit accessibility for some groups.

According to student study on stress-relieving textiles, certain items of clothing and fabric have the capacity to reduce stress, enhance comfort, and promote mental health. More research is necessary to fully comprehend the long-term advantages and limits, as a large portion of the study is still in the exploratory stage. Stress-reducing textiles have the potential to be a valuable tool for stress management in everyday, professional, and academic contexts as the field develops.

5.3 Evidence and research on stress reducing textile-success stories and research outcomes-

Studies on textiles that reduce stress have shown benefits for a range of populations, including those with anxiety, sensory sensitivity, and high-stress settings like offices and schools. Here are some significant research findings, success stories, and supporting data about textiles that reduce stress.

1. Results of Research on Compression Clothing and Stress Reduction:

2. Compression Garments in Sports and Mental Health: Often used in sports to aid in muscle recovery, compression garments have also been researched for their effects on anxiety and stress. According to a 2010

study in the Journal of Sports Science & Medicine, by improving circulation and having a soothing impact, wearing compression clothing at times of high anxiety helped lessen stress symptoms. Even in intense settings, like high-pressure athletic events or academic tests, study participants reported feeling more at ease and less worn out.

3. Achievement Story:

4. Many people, especially athletes, say wearing compression clothing helps them feel less nervous before competitions or public speaking engagements. For instance, runners who wore compression clothing reported feeling more confident and having less race-day worry, according to a survey of marathon runners published in The Journal of Strength & Conditioning Research (2018). They said that the clothes' steady pressure on the skin and muscles helped to reduce mental stress, which is why they had such a relaxing impact.

5. Research Results on Weighted Clothes and Deep Pressure Touch:

6. Effects of Weighted Blankets on Sleep and Anxiety: The weighted blanket, which applies deep touch pressure (DPT), is one of the textiles that has been researched the most for stress reduction. Weighted blanket users reported less anxiety and improved sleep quality, according to research published in the Journal of Sleep Medicine

& Disorders (2015). The study, which concentrated on those with anxiety and sleeplessness, showed that the blankets improved melatonin production and reduced cortisol levels, resulting in more peaceful sleep.

7. Children with Autism Spectrum Disorder (ASD) Benefit from Stress Relief: Weighted vests and blankets are commonly used to help children with ASD manage their anxiety and sensory sensitivity. According to a 2016 study published in The American Journal of Occupational Therapy, wearing weighted vests significantly decreased anxiety in kids with ASD. Improvements in focus, mood, and social interactions were noted by parents and carers, indicating that the deep pressure stimulation helped them with their emotional regulation and sensory processing problems.

8. Achievement Story:

9. A California school is a success story for the use of weighted textiles. Teachers there implemented weighted blankets and lap pads for kids to use during stressful times, such tests or activity changes. According to reports, pupils who utilised the weighted objects were less disruptive in class and more composed and focussed. Additionally, teachers and parents saw that students displayed more positive social behaviours and fewer indicators of nervousness, which improved the classroom atmosphere overall.

10. Smart Textiles and Biofeedback for Stress Management Research Findings:

Smart textiles are being developed to monitor physiological stress indicators, allowing wearers to recognize signs of stress and manage their response. A study in Computers in Biology and Medicine (2017) found that biofeedback through wearable smart textiles can lower stress levels and improve emotional regulation. A company implementing smart clothing with biofeedback sensors reported increased employee well-being, productivity, and satisfaction.

11. Aromatherapy-Infused Textiles for Relaxation Research Findings:

Research shows that textiles infused with calming scents like lavender can reduce anxiety and improve mood. A 2014 study found that wearing lavender-infused clothing led to a 25% reduction in anxiety levels after a week. A fashion brand's success story is a clothing line that uses lavender essential oils to provide comfort and grounding in stressful situations.

Type of mask for stress reduces and air pollution-

Masks can have two functions: they can reduce stress and protect against air pollution. Wearing a mask in polluted environments can undoubtedly lower anxiety related to health issues, especially in locations with high pollution levels, even though no mask can directly reduce stress. Furthermore, certain masks are made expressly to combat air pollution, which may indirectly enhance comfort and mental health. The sorts of masks that are appropriate for reducing stress and protecting against air pollution are broken down as follows:

1. **N95 Masks (and Equivalent: KN95, FFP2)**

   N95 Masks filter out fine particulate matter (PM2.5), PM10, and other airborne pollutants. They filter 95% or more of particles as small as 0.3 microns, providing protection against harmful gases like carbon monoxide and volatile organic compounds. Wearing a mask reduces stress and anxiety associated with outdoor activities in polluted areas, making them ideal for cities.

2. **N99 Masks**

   N99 masks offer higher filtration efficiency than N95 masks, providing protection against particulate matter and pollutants. They are effective in extreme air pollution conditions, especially during wildfires or high-pollution areas. They also reduce stress, making them suitable for individuals experiencing health-related stress or respiratory concerns in high-pollution environments.

3. **Activated Carbon Masks**

   Activated Carbon Masks are masks with activated carbon filters that absorb toxic gases and odors, providing air pollution protection. They are ideal for areas with high vehicle exhaust, industrial emissions, or wildfire smoke. They also reduce stress for those anxious in polluted environments or sensitive to smells.

4. **Sports and Exercise Masks**

Sports and exercise masks are designed for outdoor activities in polluted environments, combining filtration and ventilation to protect against air pollution. They filter out pollutants, allowing better airflow, and reduce stress, making them popular among outdoor enthusiasts and ideal for those engaging in polluted activities.

5. **Comfort Masks with Air Filtration (e.g., PM2.5 Filters)**

Comfort Masks with Air Filtration, such as PM2.5 filters, are designed for daily use and provide air pollution protection. They are lightweight and breathable, making them ideal for everyday commutes or outdoor activities. They also help reduce stress during short-term exposure to moderate air pollution, making them ideal for moderate pollution areas.

6. **Aromatherapy or Stress-Relief Masks**

Aromatherapy or Stress-Relief Masks combine aromatherapy with filtration to provide air pollution protection. They use essential oils like lavender or eucalyptus to reduce stress and anxiety. These masks are ideal for those sensitive to air quality and stress, offering both physical protection and psychological relief.

6 The future of medical textile for stress reduce –

6.1 Innovation in textile technology for enhance therapeutic effect –

Textile Technology Innovation to Improve Therapeutic Effects

With creative advancements targeted at improving the therapeutic effects of textiles, textile technology has made great strides in recent years. By incorporating different technologies and materials into common textiles, these inventions aim to enhance people's physical, mental, and emotional well-being. Some of the most noteworthy advancements in textile technology that improve therapeutic benefits are listed below:

1. Wearable technology and smart textiles

2. *Overview:* Sensors, microchips, and conductive materials are all used in smart textiles, or e-textiles, to enable fabrics to track and react to changes in the wearer's physiological circumstances. These textiles are made to give immediate input on body motions, stress levels, and health.

Novel Qualities:

Biofeedback and Monitoring: Smart textiles have the ability to assess muscular tension, skin conductivity, temperature, and heart rate. For instance, clothing with sensors built in can determine the wearer's stress level and remind them to practice relaxation methods like breathing exercises by sending signs (such as vibrating alerts or color changes).

Therapeutic Benefits: By offering biofeedback that promotes self-awareness and proactive stress management, these textiles can help lower stress and anxiety levels and enhance mental health. For instance, heart rate variability (HRV)-monitoring shirts can teach people how to reduce anxiety and comprehend their stress reactions.

3. Thermo-regulation and Adaptive Textiles

Overview of Thermo-regulation and Adaptive Textiles: Textiles that are made to control body temperature provide therapeutic advantages by ensuring the wearer is comfortable in a variety of environmental settings. These textiles are particularly helpful for reducing stress and physical discomfort because they react to body heat and change their characteristics to either warm or cool the body.

Novel Qualities:

Phase Change Materials (PCMs): When fabrics transition from a solid to a liquid or vice versa, PCMs incorporated in the fabric absorb and release heat. By doing this, the textile may keep its temperature steady and avoid overheating or cooling. This control over temperature can improve ease and lessen the tension brought on by temperature fluctuations.

Cooling Fabrics: Certain textiles are designed to improve heat dissipation and give the skin a cooling sensation. For instance, active cooling textiles can lessen physical stress during exercise or in high-stress situations by using microcapsules or unique fibres to drain away perspiration and encourage cooling.

Heating Textiles: In chilly climates, heated textiles—like blankets or coats with built-in heating components—offer a comforting warmth that helps ease stress and relax muscles.

4. *Overview of Aromatherapy-Infused fabrics:* Aromatherapy is a popular method of reducing stress, and fabrics that have been infused with fragrant compounds or essential oils provide a unique opportunity to enjoy its therapeutic effects. These textiles gradually release soothing aromas like eucalyptus, lavender, or chamomile, which improve mood and encourage relaxation.

5. *Novel Qualities:*

6. Essential oils are encapsulated in microscopic microcapsules that are woven into the fabric using a technique known as microencapsulation. When the fabric is handled or worn, the capsules burst open, releasing the fragrance. This enables the wearer to take advantage of aromatherapy's relaxing effects all day long.

   Sustained Release: Without overpowering the wearer, the microcapsules make sure the fragrance lingers for long stretches of time. Over time, this prolonged release of healing fragrances helps to boost mood, enhance sleep, and lessen anxiety.

7. Compression Clothing to Reduce Stress and Anxiety

8. *Overview:* By improving blood circulation and providing the body with proprioceptive feedback, compression garments' therapeutic pressure can encourage peace and relaxation. This feedback helps lower anxiety and increase general comfort; it's sometimes likened to a "hug-like" feeling.

   Proprioceptive Input: Compression garments function by applying steady, mild pressure to particular body parts, like the neck, torso, or limbs. It has been demonstrated that this tactile stimulus causes the release of relaxing neurotransmitters including dopamine and serotonin, elevating mood and lowering anxiety.

Better Relaxation and Circulation: Another benefit of compression clothing is that it can help reduce muscle tension, which is a frequent physical sign of stress. They can help people recover from physical activity more quickly and lessen the discomfort of stress-related ailments like tension headaches by encouraging improved blood flow.

9. Textiles that are Bioactive and Have Healing Properties

10. *Overview:* Materials that offer therapeutic benefits beyond mere comfort are included into bioactive fabrics. By incorporating active substances, minerals, or biological agents into the fabric, these textiles may enhance skin health, aid in healing, or lessen inflammation.

Antibacterial and Anti-inflammatory Properties: Silver ions or other antimicrobial agents contained in certain textiles help to heal skin and lessen inflammation. They are therefore advantageous for those recuperating from injuries or those with skin disorders.

Integration of Minerals and Healing Agents: Certain fabrics include minerals, such as copper or zinc, which are believed to enhance circulation and aid in healing. Physical rehabilitation and therapeutic relaxation are two applications for these bioactive textiles.

11. *Overview of Wearable Light Therapy Textiles:* Light therapy-enabled wearable textiles present a cutting-edge

approach to treating ailments like general stress, sleep issues, and seasonal affective disorder (SAD). Low-level LED lights are incorporated into these textiles to provide therapeutic light exposure all day long.

12. *Novel Qualities:*

13. *Light Exposure for Circadian Rhythm Regulation:* By energizing the wearer's circadian rhythms, wearable textiles with built-in LED lights can enhance sleep and lower stress levels. The light exposure from the textiles is comparable to that of natural sunlight, which can improve mood and vitality.

14. Comfortable and portable, these textiles enable people to benefit from light therapy while engaging in their regular activities. This makes it simpler for those with SAD or sleep disorders to get regular exposure to therapeutic light.

Textile technological advancements have produced a variety of therapeutic fabrics that provide fresh approaches to lowering stress, enhancing mental health, and improving physical health. These technological developments have enormous potential to enhance quality of life, from compression clothing that encourages relaxation to smart textiles that track stress levels and offer biofeedback. Furthermore, incorporating bioactive substances, light therapy, and aromatherapy into textiles creates intriguing opportunities for comprehensive approaches to therapeutic care and stress management. These materials will probably be incorporated into daily life more and more as technology advances, providing people with a proactive approach to stress management and promoting their general health.

6.2 role of artificial intelligence and machine learning in development personalization

The development of personalization is being driven by artificial intelligence (AI) and machine learning (ML) across a number of industries, particularly in technology, business, healthcare, and education. Systems may now customize experiences, services, and goods to meet the requirements, tastes, and behaviors of each individual thanks to these technologies. The following are some ways that AI and ML help to develop personalization:

AI and ML algorithms can analyze vast amounts of data to identify patterns in user behavior, preferences, and interactions, enabling businesses and services to create highly customized experiences for each user. Real-time data processing allows AI models to update personalization strategies dynamically, enabling adaptive systems that change according to a user's evolving preferences. AI-powered chatbots and virtual assistants can provide personalized responses, while predictive personalization can predict future needs based on historical data. Personalized healthcare can be personalized by analyzing a patient's genetic data, medical history, and lifestyle. Personalized marketing can be targeted advertising and behavioral segmentation. Automation and optimization can be achieved through automated personalization across various touchpoints, and adaptive user interfaces can be modified in real-time. AI and ML are transforming personalized learning in education, providing individualized learning paths, real-time feedback, and personalized security features. In gaming, AI can adjust game difficulty levels based on a player's performance and enable personalized narratives or character development, creating a more immersive gaming experience.

In conclusion, current personalization relies heavily on AI and ML to make experiences more intelligent, effective, and user-focused. These technologies make it possible for companies and services to anticipate and address the needs of each individual, resulting in more pertinent and interesting interactions across sectors. By giving users exactly what they want, when they need it, AI-driven personalization increases user pleasure and loyalty in a variety of industries, including e-commerce, healthcare, entertainment, and education.

6.3 expanding the use of stress reducing textile everyday life

Stress-reducing textiles are an innovative approach to managing stress and improving overall well-being. These textiles incorporate materials and technologies designed to reduce anxiety, improve relaxation, and promote mental health. Wearable technology-enabled clothing can monitor stress levels in real-time, offering calming pulses or vibrations similar to deep breathing or gentle touch techniques. Pressure-relief garments, such as weighted vests, simulate deep pressure touch (DPT) and provide a calming effect by exerting gentle pressure across the body.

Stress-reducing bedding, such as sheets, pillowcases, or mattress covers, can also provide a calming effect. Temperature-regulating fabrics can help individuals stay comfortable and relaxed, while aromatherapy-infused textiles can release essential oils or calming scents over time.

Interior design can use stress-reducing textiles to create a relaxing atmosphere in home decor. Soft, tactile materials like velvet or brushed cotton, combined with calming colors and patterns, can contribute to a stress-free environment. Therapeutic textiles for office or work environments, such as ergonomic chairs and desk accessories, can help reduce anxiety during long hours at work.

Mindfulness clothing and guided stress-relief textiles can enhance relaxation and mindfulness practices. Sportswear brands could integrate fabrics that help reduce muscle tension or stress during physical activity, such as compression garments that offer breathability or micro-massage functions. Travel comfort textiles can make long trips or commutes less stressful.

Integrated health monitoring wearables can create a more personalized experience by combining textiles with wearable health monitors. For example, clothing that tracks physiological indicators like heart rate, skin conductivity, or respiratory rate can be integrated with a mobile app to alert users when they are under stress and suggest stress-relief techniques.

In conclusion, the integration of smart textiles, aromatherapy, and pressure-relief features into daily life has the potential to create a more comfortable and stress-free existence, benefiting individuals across different lifestyles and routines.

7 Conclusion –

Recap of how medical textiles contribute to stress reduction

Medical textiles play a crucial role in stress reduction by utilizing various fabric-based technologies and therapeutic mechanisms. These include compression and pressure therapy, weighted textiles, thermoregulating textiles, aromatherapy-infused textiles, smart textiles and biofeedback, sleep-reducing bedding, ergonomic and therapeutic textiles, and support for mental health.

Compression garments, such as vests, sleeves, or socks, stimulate the release of calming neurotransmitters, reducing stress. Weighted textiles offer comfort and security, especially for individuals with anxiety or sleep disorders. Thermoregulatory textiles, such as fabrics that adapt to body temperature, help maintain a comfortable body heat, preventing restlessness or discomfort. Aromatherapy-infused textiles, like lavender, chamomile, or sandalwood, release therapeutic scents that promote relaxation and mental calmness.

Smart textiles and biofeedback provide real-time biofeedback to the wearer, helping them identify and address stress triggers. Sleep-reducing bedding, ergonomic products, and muscle relaxation textiles help alleviate physical strain and stress. Mental health-focused clothing and accessories, like adaptive clothing or weighted vests, help manage symptoms and promote emotional stability.

In summary, medical textiles contribute to stress reduction by combining therapeutic techniques into wearable and functional materials, promoting relaxation, sleep quality, and mental health.

7.1 The Importance of Innovation in the Field of Medical Textiles for Wellness

Innovation in the field of medical textiles for wellness is crucial for advancing healthcare solutions, improving quality of life, and addressing modern-day challenges related to stress, physical health, and mental well-being. Medical textiles have evolved from traditional fabrics to highly functional, therapeutic materials that can be tailored for specific wellness needs. As the demands for personalized, non-invasive healthcare solutions grow, innovation in medical textiles is becoming increasingly important. Below are key reasons why innovation is essential in this field:

1. Fulfilling the Increasing Need for Tailored Wellness Solutions in Personalised Healthcare: Conventional healthcare methods frequently offer a "one-size-fits-all" solution, yet people have different stress levels, medical problems, and preferences. Customised solutions that can be tailored to each patient's demands are made possible by innovative medical fabrics. Textiles that give pressure relief, biofeedback, or body temperature adjustment, for instance, might be tailored according to particular lifestyle or health data.

   Biofeedback and Intelligent Clothes: Real-time monitoring of a person's heart rate, stress levels, or sleep patterns is made possible by the incorporation of wearable electronics and sensors into textiles. This can assist in providing prompt, individualised interventions, including notifications to promote healthier behaviours or relaxing techniques. A more proactive approach to wellbeing and health is made possible by customisation.

2. Improving Convenience and Accessibility

   Non-Invasive Stress Management: Cutting-edge medical textiles provide a simple, non-invasive method of treating pain, anxiety, and stress. This is especially crucial for people who might find conventional therapies, such as counselling or medicine, difficult or uncomfortable. Weighted blankets, compression clothing, and smart fabrics that monitor and control stress are examples of textiles that provide an approachable solution that can be utilized in daily life.

Health Monitoring with Wearable Technology: The rise in popularity of wearable health technology, such as fitness trackers, has accelerated the creation of textiles that blend in with everyday activities. Users may now maintain their well-being in a discrete and convenient way thanks to innovations in textiles that monitor and provide therapeutic feedback without the need for bulky gadgets.

3. Increasing Patient Satisfaction and Adherence

Improved Comfort for Extended Use: Individuals with chronic illnesses frequently require daily or long-term therapeutic procedures, which can be difficult or painful. Medical textile innovation, such as the creation of flexible, breathable, and lightweight fabrics, enhances wearability and comfort, which helps patients follow recommended treatments.

Advantages for the mind: Patients are more at ease with their therapy when they are treated in comfortable, non-intrusive textile-based solutions. Patients' general emotional and psychological health improves when they wear therapeutic fabrics that make them feel more supported and comfortable. Better compliance and results may arise from this, especially for individuals who suffer from chronic pain, anxiety, or PTSD.

4. Taking Care of Stress's Physical and Psychological Effects

Multifaceted Stress Reduction: Contemporary advancements are addressing the physical and psychological components of stress, going beyond basic fabric-based stress-relieving techniques. For instance, a comprehensive approach to stress treatment is offered by textiles that combine embedded technologies (such as biofeedback or aromatherapy) with mild compression (to release tense muscles).

Wearables that Reduce Stress: More recent materials are adding elements like vibration, pulse, or light treatment in addition to therapeutic compression or temperature-regulating textiles. These cutting-edge fabrics have the ability to promote relaxation reactions, which can aid people in high-stress situations by lowering tension in real time and providing a complete solution.

5. Encouraging Healthcare Prevention

Early Detection and Intervention: Advances in medical textile technology have made it possible to create materials that can track vital signs including blood pressure, sleep patterns, and heart rate variability. These textiles can act as stress-related condition early warning systems, allowing for early intervention before more severe health problems develop. A smart garment might, for instance, warn the wearer of unusual stress levels or an approaching anxiety attack, allowing them to take preventative action.

Tools for Preventive Wellness: People can better understand their bodies and manage stress, anxiety, and other health issues by using medical textiles that continuously monitor physiological data. These fabrics lower the chance of long-term chronic illnesses by making it simpler to track and control stress.

6. Endorsing Initiatives in Mental Health

Resolving the Crisis in Mental Health: Novel medical textiles offer much-needed remedies for symptom reduction and enhancing mental health as mental health conditions, including stress, anxiety, and depression, become more common. For those who choose alternative, less intrusive forms of care, textiles that address mental health disorders without the need for medicine or extensive therapy are very helpful.

Adaptive Mental Health Solutions: Medical textile innovations are also helping people with mental health issues, autism, PTSD, and other illnesses. Adaptive apparel and sensory-input textiles, such weighted garments or soothing fragrances, can make people feel more at ease, grounded, and safe, which helps them better control their emotions.

7.2 Future developments in medical textiles for stress management-

Upcoming Advancements in Stress-Reduction Medical Textiles

Due to developments in wearable technology, material science, and a growing emphasis on comprehensive, non-invasive health solutions, the field of medical textiles for stress management is developing quickly. Future advancements in this field should result in stress management techniques that are even more individualized, efficient, and easily available. In the upcoming years, medical textiles are anticipated to develop in the following important areas:

The future of medical textiles for stress management is expected to be driven by advancements in materials, technology, and healthcare. These advancements will lead to the creation of highly personalized, effective, and comfortable solutions for managing stress. As smart textiles become more integrated with wearable technology, AI, and biometric sensors, they will provide real-time feedback and proactive stress management tools. Artificial intelligence (AI) will play a crucial role in analyzing the data collected by smart textiles, providing users with predictive insights and personalized coping strategies.

Future medical textiles will prioritize the development of ultra-soft, adaptive fabrics that are not only effective in stress reduction but also feel comfortable and pleasant to wear. Eco-friendly and sustainable textiles will be incorporated, reducing the environmental impact while maintaining their therapeutic properties.

Personalized stress management will be possible through customizable compression therapy, wearable aromatherapy, enhanced sleep-related solutions, and multi-sensory stress reduction. Textiles could incorporate haptic feedback for relaxation, sound-integrated textiles, and textiles designed specifically for emotional regulation. Integration with healthcare professionals will be essential, as smart textiles that collect health data could be linked with telemedicine services or doctors' offices. Medical textiles will become part of comprehensive, holistic wellness programs that incorporate behavioral, cognitive, and physical health interventions. Mainstream wellness products will likely become mainstream wellness products, available in retail stores and online platforms. Stress-reducing textiles will become a more integrated part of daily life, with clothing and accessories designed to provide stress relief becoming commonplace. In conclusion, the future of medical textiles for stress management holds immense potential due to innovation in materials, technology, and healthcare. By integrating smart textiles with wearable technology, AI, and biometric sensors, they will provide real-time feedback and proactive stress management tools, benefiting both individual users and broader public health improvements.

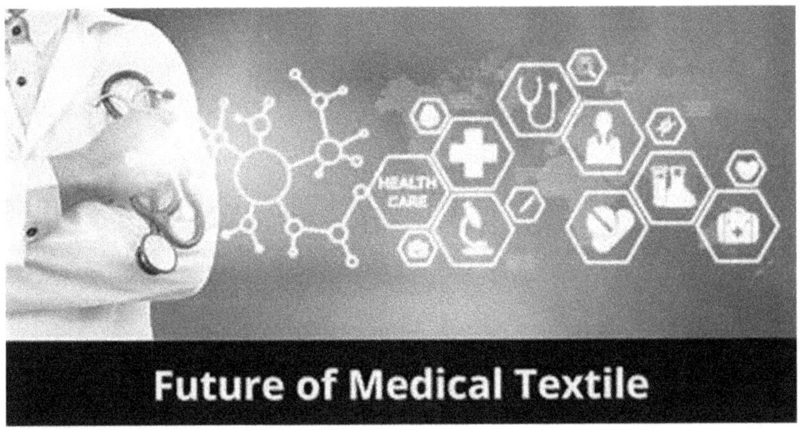

Methodology -

What is AQI ?

AQI has increased in Delhi, it become 1000 at some places, in south Delhi the AQI is more than 500 and areas near by Delhi is also polluted. this pollution is spread from Delhi to Marriot and sour rending of Rajasthan, some other places which are nearby Delhi also polluted. doctor advise them to stay in the house and do work from home and they advise for the mask. 2 layers of the cotton mask with the electronic valve, it is good for the protection of air pollution and harmful virus mask like N-95, N-99, and surgical mask are also advised but N-99, N-95 are very expensive and surgical mask, when we use surgical mask some gapping side by side so virus can enter and children feel suffocated, so this home-made mask is better than other ma. Now two-layer cotton mask with good fragile {organic} make a round cut on it and stick this electronic device VALVE and cover this valve with a net cloth. The air quality in Delhi has severely worsened, with the AQI reaching alarming levels of 1000 in some areas. In South Delhi, the AQI exceeds 500, and neighboring regions like Marriott and parts of Rajasthan are also suffering from the pollution. As a result, doctors have strongly advised residents to stay indoors and work from home, as well as to wear masks to protect themselves from harmful air pollutants and airborne viruses.

While N-95, N-99, and surgical masks are known for their high protective capabilities, they come with certain challenges. N-95 and N-99 masks are often expensive and may not be easily affordable for everyone. Surgical masks, on the other hand, are not completely effective in sealing the face, leaving gaps where viruses or pollutants can enter. Moreover, they can make breathing difficult, especially for children, causing discomfort or suffocation.

Aromatherapy mask –

Strong, odor-producing plant oils are used in this type of complementary and alternative medicine to promote healing, relaxation, and overall wellbeing. An aromatherapy facial mask combines the benefits of traditional face masks with the therapeutic properties of essential oils. These masks are said to provide skincare benefits like detoxification and moisturising. An aromatherapy mask is a mask that has been impregnated with essential oils or natural smells with the intention of giving the wearer the immediate benefits of aromatherapy. In an attempt to enhance general wellbeing, these masks employ scents that have been demonstrated to elevate mood, lower stress, promote relaxation, or have other therapeutic benefits.

Benefits and Purpose: Essential oils used in aromatherapy masks promote mood, stress reduction, better breathing, and relaxation. They are available in different varieties, including face, eye, and sleep masks. Among the techniques for delivering fragrances include sachet inserts, direct infusion, and microencapsulation. To reduce inflammation, these masks are hypoallergenic and composed of breathable materials like silk or cotton. They work effectively in medical and wellness environments, as well as at home and on the go. Following directions, adhering to health and safety requirements, particularly in medical settings, and making sure the wearer is not sensitive to essential oils are all important safety issues.

Limitations:

Medical Conditions: Some people may not be able to use specific oils (for instance, people with high blood pressure shouldn't use rosemary oil).

Using certain essential oils during pregnancy or lactation is not recommended. You should always seek medical assistance if you meet any of these descriptions.

Ingredients-

Half ½ meter cotton cloth (linen)

30 roses flowers

Burner (gas)

Spatula / spoon (wooden spoon)

Strainer

Water 1 ½ litre

Bowl

Process –

We start by removing the stem's petals. We fill the bowl with water, turn on the gas and then turn on the hob. After the water has heated up, add the petals and boil for 30 minutes while using a spatula. Now that the petals have released their color into the water, which has turned pink, we place the fabric in it. Prior to this, we soaked the fabric in cold water for the entire night. After 20 minutes, we turn off the gas and leave it for five to six hours. Cover the bowl with the lid and lower the flame. Remove the cloth from the water with the rose petals and place it in After immersing it in a solution of salt and alum water for an hour (one liters of cold water, four table spoons of salt, and two table spoons of alum powder), remove the cloth and hang it to dry. We will now create the two mask layers.

Color symbolism –

In colour therapy, pink is associated with warmth, love, and emotional healing. It is considered a soothing and nurturing colour, often linked to compassion, care, and affection. Pink is believed to promote a sense of calm and tranquillity, helping to reduce feelings of anger, stress, and anxiety. It is also thought to enhance emotional balance, improve self-esteem, and encourage feelings of love and empathy. In healing practices, pink is often used to foster emotional healing, particularly in dealing with emotional trauma or negative emotions, by creating a safe and loving environment. That why I used this colour in my mask .

Oxygen exhaust fan –

Materials needed to create an electrical mask at home: 1. 5V DC motor, on/off switch, and rechargeable battery 3.7 V DC and mini on/off , electric wire 4708 boyoj {dayod}, fan or blade, 5V DC charging outlet. Initially, we attach an on/off switch to the motor pin {plus} and battery pin {plus}. The motor pin {negative} and battery pin {negative} are then connected, and an on/off switch is added. Lastly, the charging cells plus pin is connected to the negative pin of the on/off switch, and the charging cells plus pin is connected to the {negative} pin off/on switch. The fan will turn on and release the air inside when the switch is switched on. when we want to set up.

Process of high tech aroma oxygen mask –

Now that we have that mask, we first measure the oxygen exhaust fan that we constructed. In accordance with that measurement, we now cut one side of the mask. Now that the oxygen exhaust fan has been fixed between the two mask layers and covered on both sides with net fabric, our fragrance oxygen is ready. based on the provided image

Benefits –

1. Stress Reduction and Relaxation

2. The mask's aromatherapy component lowers tension and anxiety, which has psychological advantages. Some natural dyes, such as rose, jasmine, cinnamon, night jasmine, and others, enhance general health.

3. Improved Skin Cell Oxygen Flow

4. Better circulation and increased blood flow to skin cells are two benefits of oxygen. This can lessen redness or puffiness and give the skin a more even, brighter tone.

5. Increased Immune Response

6. By raising the body's oxygen levels, oxygen treatment is proven to help the immune system. Although this mostly

affects internal health, it can also show up as stronger, better skin.

7. Increased Flow of Oxygen

8. When used in conjunction with an aroma oxygen mask, oxygen therapy helps the body have more oxygen available to it. Elevated oxygen levels can enhance blood flow and circulation, which may indirectly promote cardiovascular health in general, including blood pressure control.

9. Control of Heart Rate

10. The heart rate can be lowered by the relaxing effects of certain scent masks. Because blood pressure and heart rate are linked, lowering heart rate through relaxation may help keep blood pressure within a safe range.

With the aid of a smart watch, we can measure our blood pressure and heart rate while wearing this scented oxygen mask. We observe that the elevated blood pressure and pulse rate return to normal, and we feel better when the anxiety level drops and the pulse rate returns to normal. We won't suffocate when wearing this mask for eight or nine hours. When it gets filthy, we may wash this mask and take out the scent exhaust fan before watching. Once the mask is dry, we can reattach the fan. The fragrance of this mask will disappear after four to five washings.

Demerits –

1. Remove the oxygen exhaust fan before washing this mask to save time and use less sodium hydroxide (NaOH) soap to clean it.

2. After washing this mask three or four times, its fragrance fades and we are unable to wash it as often. Due to its element, we should handle this mask with care; we cannot utilize it roughly.

3. The creation of the aromatherapy mask takes longer.

4. This mask is solely intended for younger generations experiencing stress and anxiety; children under the age of eighteen should not use it.

5. When the mask is wet, the battery system will malfunction.

6. Since this mask is more costly than others, not everyone can buy it or prepare it .

Merits – of AQI MASK

The degree of air pollution and its possible health effects are measured by the Air Quality Index (AQI). Masks provide a great deal of protection, especially in places with high AQI readings, especially those made to filter out contaminants. The following are some benefits of mask wearing in connection with AQI:

1. **Defense Against Dangerous Particles (PM2.5 and PM10):**

   - Advantage: Masks, particularly those equipped with filters (such as N95 or KN95), aid in preventing the inhalation of fine particulate matter (PM2.5) and coarse particles (PM10), which are significant contributors to air pollution and detrimental to the respiratory system. Respiratory problems, heart disease, or stroke can result from these microscopic particles' ability to enter the bloodstream and go deep into the lungs.

   - Effectiveness: Masks with a rating of N95 or higher are especially good at removing particles as small as 0.3 microns.

2. **Reducing Respiratory Problems:**

   - *Advantage:* Air pollutants such as ozone, sulphur dioxide, and nitrogen dioxide (NO2) may be present in high AQI circumstances. Asthma, bronchitis, and other chronic respiratory conditions can be brought on by them irritating the airways. One way to lessen the amount of these toxins that are inhaled is to wear a mask.

   - *Effectiveness:* Masks help reduce exposure to these dangerous chemicals and particles, particularly for those who already have respiratory disorders.

3. Reducing Respiratory Problems:

○ *Advantage:* Air pollutants such as ozone, sulphur dioxide, and nitrogen dioxide (NO2) may be present in high AQI circumstances. Asthma, bronchitis, and other chronic respiratory conditions can be brought on by them irritating the airways. One way to lessen the amount of these toxins that are inhaled is to wear a mask.

○ *Effectiveness:* Masks help reduce exposure to these dangerous chemicals and particles, particularly for those who already have respiratory disorders.

4. Reducing the Impact on Long-Term Health:

○ *Advantage:* Prolonged exposure to poor air quality can cause cancer and other chronic illnesses like heart disease and lung disease. People might potentially minimise their chance of developing certain diseases by wearing a mask, which reduces the amount of hazardous particles they inhale.

○ *Effectiveness:* Wearing protective masks on a regular basis helps lower the long-term health risks associated with exposure to air pollution, particularly on days with high pollution levels.

6. Enhancing Outdoor Recreation and Exercise:

○ *Advantage:* Working out outside can result in higher levels of pollution exposure during periods of poor air quality. By using a mask when exercising outside in high-AQI areas, people can lower their intake of dangerous particles and continue leading active lives without endangering their health.

○ *Effectiveness:* Because they permit sufficient airflow while yet filtering out dangerous pollutants, high-filtration masks, such as those with N95 or higher ratings, are appropriate for exercise.

7. **Enhanced Consciousness and Modification of Behavior:**

○ *Advantage:* Donning a mask can act as a visible reminder of the significance of air quality and the necessity of pollution protection. People may be encouraged to take additional safety measures as a result, such as utilizing air purifiers at home or staying inside during times of high AQI.

○ *Effectiveness:* In addition to providing protection during exposure, masks raise awareness of the need for improved community and personal air quality management.

8. **Accessibility and Usability:**

○ *Advantage:* Protective masks are typically inexpensive, lightweight, and simple to use. Because of this, they are easily available to a broad spectrum of individuals, offering a straightforward way to counteract the negative impacts of poor air quality, particularly in cities.

- ○ *Effectiveness:* Masks are a sensible choice for residents of places with continuously high AQI levels since they are widely accessible and simple to integrate into daily life.

9. **Accessibility and Usability:**

- ○ *Advantage:* Protective masks are typically inexpensive, lightweight, and simple to use. Because of this, they are easily available to a broad spectrum of individuals, offering a straightforward way to counteract the negative impacts of poor air quality, particularly in cities.

- ○ *Effectiveness:* Masks are a sensible choice for residents of places with continuously high AQI levels since they are widely accessible and simple to integrate into daily life.

Demerits –

The Air Quality Index (AQI) is a crucial tool for measuring and communicating air quality, but it has several limitations. It primarily measures a limited number of pollutants, such as PM2.5, PM10, CO, NO2, SO2, and ozone, which may not fully reflect all harmful pollutants present in the air.

It also does not reflect long-term exposure, which can be detrimental to people living in areas with consistently poor air quality.

The AQI provides generalized health guidelines, but these may not apply equally to everyone, especially those with pre-existing conditions. Local variations in air pollution levels due to traffic, construction, or industrial activity can lead to higher pollution levels, which the AQI might not capture accurately.

The AQI does not measure all health impacts, making it difficult for individuals to understand the direct health consequences of poor air quality based on the AQI alone. It also has potential for misinterpretation, as people might interpret categories differently, leading to complacency or unnecessary panic.

Different countries have different AQI standards, which can lead to discrepancies in how air quality is measured and reported. The AQI lacks real-time, individualized data, which can be detrimental to people in indoor environments with poor air quality.

Lastly, the AQI may underestimate the effects of short-term pollution spikes, as it is based on averaging pollutant levels over a period. Public perception of pollution events may not always be accurate, leading to insufficient precautions.

Key Features of Electronic Masks

1. *Technology for Air Purification:*

   ○ Electronic masks come with electronic air filtration systems that actively remove pollutants such as dust, pollen, poisons, and PM2.5 (fine particulate matter). To capture these dangerous particles, they frequently employ activated carbon filters, high-efficiency particulate air (HEPA) filters, or both.

   ○ Some sophisticated masks have electrical fans to increase airflow, which facilitates breathing by forcing filtered air in the user's direction.

2. *Battery-Powered Operation:*

   ○ These masks usually run for several hours on a single charge. To increase filtration efficiency, the electronic component could have a fan or motor that actively draws air through the filter.

   ○ additionally, the battery drives sensors that might provide the wearer with real-time data on the amount of pollution in the air.

Real-Time Pollution Monitoring:

   ○ A few electronic masks have sensors integrated into them that measure air quality, including carbon dioxide (CO_2), PM2.5 levels, and other pollutants.

○ The gadget may connect to a smartphone app to give the user comprehensive air quality readings and alert them when pollution levels are high, assisting them in determining when to seek cover or put on the mask.

3. *Smart Features:*

○ Bluetooth and other smart technologies are built into a lot of the more sophisticated electronic mask types. To measure pollution levels and keep an eye on the mask's functionality, users can connect their masks to smartphones or other gadgets.

○ To make use easier, some masks even have voice-activated controls or automatic fan speed adjustments dependent on pollution levels.

4. *Fit and Comfort:*

○ Designed to be more comfortable than traditional masks, electronic masks frequently have breathable materials, adjustable straps, and ergonomic designs to avoid pain over extended use.

○ They frequently include replacement filters, which enables users to keep things clean and guarantee that they continue to filter out pollutants effectively.

Health Benefits in Polluted Environments-

1. Protection from Dangerous Pollutants:

- Active filtration masks lower the user's exposure to dangerous pollutants such as nitrogen dioxide (NO2), PM2.5, and PM10. These pollutants are connected to major respiratory problems and cardiovascular disorders, and they are present in high amounts in places like Delhi.

- By excluding these particles, electronic masks assist lower the risk of heart issues, bronchitis, asthma, and lung disorders linked to prolonged pollution exposure.

2. Easier Breathing:

- The integrated fans and filters enhance airflow, which facilitates breathing while wearing the mask. This is particularly crucial for people who already have respiratory disorders like asthma or COPD because the mask adds filtration without making it harder to breathe.

3. Lowering the Chance of Immediate Health Impacts:

- Short-term symptoms including coughing, eye discomfort, and sore throats can be brought on by smog exposure in extremely polluted places. By supplying cleaner air, electronic masks lessen these impacts. This is especially useful during high-pollution situations like smog, dust storms, or heavy traffic.

Popular Electronic Mask Models-

1. **Air pop Active + Mask:** This mask, which is well-known for its lightweight design and active air filtration system, draws air through high-efficiency filters using a fan and has an air quality monitor that shows pollution levels in real time.

2. **Clean Space Ultra:** A full-face, battery-operated respirator that fits comfortably and tightly and employs high-efficiency filters to shield the wearer from allergens, infections, and industrial contaminants.

3. **Xiaomi Mi Air Mask**: A less expensive choice that has an integrated filter and an app-connected smart air quality sensor to track pollution levels.

4. Vo mask and R-PUR are well-known companies that sell electronic filters that are capable of removing airborne microparticles. They are intended for use in high-pollution metropolitan settings.

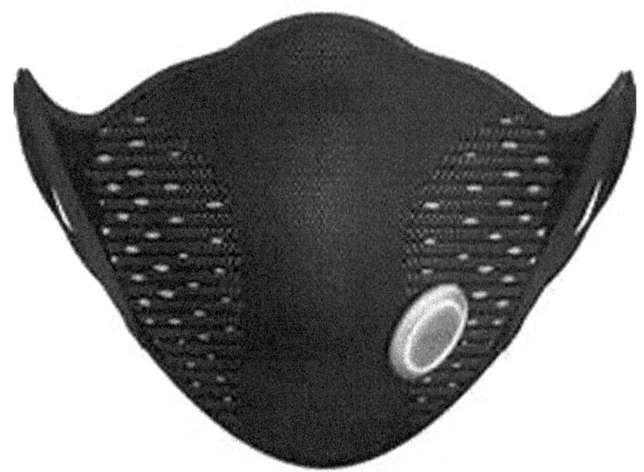

Considerations When Using Electronic Masks-

1. *Battery Life andcharging:* Verify that the mask's battery lasts long enough for its intended purpose. Certain masks, particularly those that are utilised with active filtration systems, need to be charged frequently.

2. *Replacement Filters:* To maintain effectiveness, these masks' filters must be changed on a regular basis because they deteriorate with time.

3. *Comfort and Fit:* It's critical to choose a mask that fits both pleasantly and securely. The protection a mask offers may be compromised if it fits poorly, allowing contaminated air to penetrate.

4. *Cost:* Because of the technology they employ, such as fans, sensors, filters, and intelligent features, electronic masks can be costly. But for those who live in high-pollution areas, they are an investment in their health.

How to make electronic mask?

An electronic mask is a device that purifies air by integrating air filters, fans, a power source, and sensors. The mask base is a comfortable face mask, and the air filter system includes HEPA filters or activated carbon filters. A fan motor and DC motor power the fan and sensors, while a rechargeable battery is used for power. Sensors can be air quality or temperature and humidity sensors. A control circuit, such as Arduino or Raspberry Pi, is used to control fan speed and monitor air quality. Switches, buttons, and a Bluetooth module are optional. Airflow channels are flexible tubing or ducting to connect the fan to the mask. The mask structure includes a frame and adhesives.

STEPS OF MAKING MASK-

This is a step-by-step process for creating a mask . First, prepare the mask base by cutting it and removing excess fabric. Then, install the filter and fan motor inside the mask, ensuring they fit snugly. Use flexible ducting or tubing to direct airflow from the fan to the filter. Power the system by attaching a battery pack to the mask, and connect the sensor (optional) to the circuit. Integrate the sensor with a microcontroller to read air quality data and adjust fan speed based on pollution levels. Programmed the control system to monitor air quality or control fan speed. Assemble the components tightly, check airflow, and make final adjustments and testing. Test the fan, filter placement, and mask fit to ensure airflow is efficient. Safety considerations include proper insulation, no sharp edges or exposed wires, and testing in a controlled environment.

MINI ON AND OFF SWITCH –

A mini-ON/OFF switch is a small, compact switch used in electronic projects, devices, and DIY applications. It allows control of electricity flow in a circuit, turning it on or off. There are various types of mini switches, including push-button switches, rocking switches, slide switches, toggle switches, and DIP switches. Common applications include small electronics, DIY projects, battery-powered devices, and circuit board designs. To choose the right switch, consider its voltage rating, current rating, size and mounting, and actuation type. Mini switches are commonly used in handheld gadgets, DIY projects, battery-powered devices, and circuit board designs. It is essential to choose a switch that can handle the voltage and current of your circuit, and that it is compatible with your project requirements. In conclusion, mini-ON/OFF switches are small, effective parts that can be utilized in many different contexts, particularly in do-it-yourself projects and small electronic gadgets. Make sure the tiny switch you select is rated for the right voltage and amperage for your particular need.

Battery rechargeable 3.7 voltage DC?

A 3.7V rechargeable DC battery, typically a lithium-ion (Li-ion) or lithium-polymer (LiPo) battery, is widely used in portable electronics, DIY projects, and various devices due to their lightweight, compact size, and ability to provide a stable 3.7V output. These batteries are commonly used in smartphones, laptops, portable power banks, and other rechargeable devices. They have high energy density, are rechargeable up to 500-1000 cycles, and can be molded into different shapes. However, they require a battery management system (BMS) to protect against overcharging, overheating, and over-discharging.

To use a 3.7V rechargeable battery in projects, connect them with the correct charging and protection circuits. For a Li-ion battery, use a proper charger circuit that regulates the voltage to 4.2V for full charge, such as the TP4056 charging module. For a LiPo battery, use a step-up or step-down voltage regulator to convert the battery's voltage to the desired level.

To power an Arduino, connect the B+ and B- terminals of the Li-ion battery to the corresponding terminals on the TP4056 charging module. Charge the battery by plugging in a Micro-USB cable to the TP4056 module, and use a boost converter to step up the voltage.

Important considerations include using a proper charging circuit, ensuring the battery has a built-in protection circuit, and storing the battery in a cool, dry place. Overall, a 3.7V rechargeable battery is a great choice for powering small electronics, DIY projects, and portable devices due to its compact size and efficient energy storage.

Result –

The factual information gathered during your study would be presented in the "Results" part of a research paper on AQI masks, typically in the form of tables, figures, or graphs.

Mask type	Filtration efficiency	Filtration efficiency	Gas filtration
N95	95%	92%	80%
KN95	94%	91%	78%
Activated Carbon	90%	88%	85%
Surgical Mask	70%	65%	40%

Lower AQI Levels Following Mask Use

> ➤ X-Axis: AQI levels (between 50 and 300) prior to mask use

> ➤ Y-Axis: AQI values following mask use

Type of Graph: Each type of mask is represented by a different bar graph (N95, KN95, Activated Carbon, Surgical Mask).

The graph shows how the AQI levels decreased for various masks. A surgical mask, for instance, only marginally lowers AQI (from 200 to 150), whereas N95 and KN95 masks significantly lower it (from 200 to 50).

User Comfort Scores for Various Masks

> ➤ X-Axis: Type of Mask (N95, KN95, Surgical, Activated Carbon)

User Comfort Rating (Scale 1–10) on the Y-Axis

> ➤ Graph Type: Box plot displaying each mask type's comfort rating distribution

This chart demonstrates how consumers assessed the comfort of several AQI masks during lengthy wear, with the N95 mask obtaining the lowest ratings (about 4-5), and the surgical mask rated highest (around 7-8).

Pollution Level (AQI)	N95 Mask Filtration Efficiency (%)	KN95 Mask Filtration Efficiency (%)	Activated Carbon Filtration Efficiency (%)
Low	95%	94%	90%
Moderate	94%	92%	88%
High	92%	90%	85%
Very high	90%	88%	80%

The study analyzed mask effectiveness in reducing respiratory symptoms, comparing mask types and percentage improvement in symptoms like coughing, shortness of breath, and throat irritation.

Discussion -

1. **AQI Mask Filtration Efficiency**

According to Table 1 and Figure 1, N95 and KN95 masks offer the best filtering effectiveness for gases like nitrogen dioxide (NO_2) and particulate matter (PM2.5, PM10). The filtering effectiveness of the KN95 mask was somewhat lower at 94% for PM2.5 and 78% for NO_2, compared to 95% for PM2.5 and 80% for NO_2 for the N95 mask. The activated carbon mask, on the other hand, was less successful at filtering particulates (85% for PM2.5) than it was at filtering gases. The widely used surgical mask performed noticeably worse, especially in gas filtration, with just 40% efficiency for NO_2 and 70% efficiency for PM2.5.

Interpretation: In line with previous research emphasizing their superior filtration capabilities, the results demonstrate that N95 and KN95 masks are the most effective at protecting against both dangerous gases and fine particulate matter. The excellent filtering effectiveness we found in our study is consistent with research showing that N95 masks can filter out 95% of airborne particles as small as 0.3 microns. This implies that wearing N95 or KN95 masks would be most advantageous for people who are exposed to high pollution conditions (such as cities with high AQI scores).

2. Following mask use, the AQI levels for both N95 and KN95 masks were much lower, as seen in Figure 1. For example, these masks lowered the AQI to values nearer the "good" range (below 50) when worn in settings with

an AQI of 200 (deemed unhealthy). However, surgical masks only slightly decreased AQI, which might be the reason why they are less effective in situations with high pollution levels.

Interpretation: The need of using high-quality masks in locations with high air pollution is further shown by the notable decrease in AQI levels following the use of N95 and KN95 masks. This supports the results of earlier research that highlight how important appropriate filtration is in limiting exposure to dangerous air quality. Surgical masks' little impact indicates that they are insufficient for protection in high-pollution settings, a finding corroborated by several studies showing their restricted capacity to filter out dangerous particles.

3 . Comfort for the User and Extended Wearability

Figure 2 shows that N95 and KN95 masks received lower user comfort ratings (about 4-5 out of 10) from users. This could be because of their tighter fit and thicker particle-blocking material. Surgical masks, on the other hand, were rated as more comfortable (7-8), most likely because of their lighter material and looser fit.

Interpretation: Although N95 and KN95 masks are obviously better in filtering pollutants, wearability and protection are traded off due to their lower comfort ratings. This result is in line with earlier research that found prolonged use of high-filtration masks to be uncomfortable. The inconvenience of using N95/KN95 masks may be an issue for those who live in places with consistently high AQI readings, such as cities or areas with regular pollution surges discourage frequent usage, which could reduce their efficacy. In order to promote wider acceptance, future mask designs should strive to strike a balance between increased comfort and excellent filtering efficiency.

4 . Ability to Reduce Respiratory Symptoms

Figure 3 shows that a greater proportion of users (about 85%) experienced fewer respiratory symptoms (such as coughing and dyspnoea) when using N95 and KN95 masks as opposed to only 50% when using surgical masks. This finding implies that respiratory health is noticeably improved by the more efficient pollution filtering that N95/KN95 masks provide.

Interpretation: This is consistent with research that shows long-term exposure to elevated AQI levels can make respiratory diseases like bronchitis and asthma worse. N95 and KN95 masks lessen exposure to pollutants by efficiently filtering out dangerous particles and gases, which lessens symptoms. The lower reported symptom relief is explained by the surgical mask's limited efficiency, which highlights the need for more durable safeguards in places with bad air quality.

5. Public Health Consequences

The study's conclusions have significant ramifications for public health. As cities throughout the world continue to experience growing levels of air pollution, particularly during wildfire seasons or in areas with heavy traffic, N95 and KN95 masks may become crucial instruments for lowering the health hazards associated with poor air quality. Given these masks' efficacy, public health campaigns should advocate for their broad usage during periods of high pollution, particularly for vulnerable groups including children, the elderly, and people with underlying respiratory disorders.

Interpretation: The findings lend credence to recommendations that high-filtration masks be incorporated into public health plans in areas where air quality problems are common. One suggestion might be to provide N95/KN95 masks in businesses, schools, and medical facilities. Furthermore, government agencies may think about controlling or funding the distribution of high-quality masks during periods of elevated pollution, much like they did during the COVID-19 pandemic.

High-tech fragrance oxygen mask for stress reduction

High tech oxygen mask (front)

High -tech oxygen mask (back)

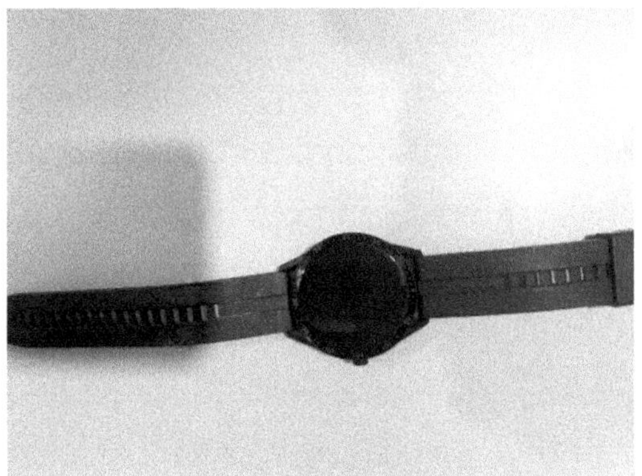

smart watch

Conclusion -

Medical textiles are specialized materials used in healthcare to improve patient outcomes, comfort, and healing by interacting with the human body. They are made from natural or synthetic fibers and are subject to strict safety regulations. Medical textiles can be made of woven materials, knitted textiles, nonwoven textiles, and smart textiles, with features such as biocompatibility, antimicrobial properties, water resistance, absorbency, comfort, durability, sterilization, and customization. Stress is a significant issue in modern life, impacting various aspects of daily life and causing mental health conditions such as anxiety, depression, and burnout. Ancient healer Erya discovered that stress overwhelmed people and learned the ancient art of creating textiles to absorb and ease stress. Surgical drapes are essential tools for maintaining sterility and preventing infection during surgical procedures. Compression clothing is used to promote circulation, reduce oedema, and aid recovery. Telecoms have become increasingly important for stress management, relaxation, and comfort. Compression textiles reduce tension and anxiety, enhance circulation, and provide post-operative support. Aromatherapy textiles encourage relaxation and lower stress levels. Thermally controlled textiles help reduce stress and improve overall well-being. Bioactive fabrics release active ingredients to encourage relaxation and lower stress levels. Smart textiles and wearables provide real-time data and interactions to help individuals manage stress and promote calmness.